THE RE-EVANGELISATION
OF ENGLAND

MACMILLAN AND CO., Limited
LONDON · BOMBAY · CALCUTTA · MADRAS
MELBOURNE

THE MACMILLAN COMPANY
NEW YORK · BOSTON · CHICAGO
DALLAS · SAN FRANCISCO

THE MACMILLAN CO. OF CANADA, Ltd.
TORONTO

THE ROMSEY CRUCIFIX.

(See p. 119 and Appendix B.)

THE
RE-EVANGELISATION
OF ENGLAND

BEING STUDIES
IN RELIGIOUS RECONSTRUCTION

BY

CYRIL HEPHER

CANON OF WINCHESTER
AUTHOR OF "THE FRUITS OF SILENCE," ETC.

MACMILLAN AND CO., LIMITED
ST. MARTIN'S STREET, LONDON
1918

TO THE MEMORY

OF

MY MOTHER

PREFACE

WHILE these pages were passing from printer to binder the din of war ceased only less suddenly than it began. Already men are setting themselves to remake the world. Reconstruction, social, national and international, might seem to demand our entire thought, and those who during the War put away the evangelistic challenge to await a more convenient season will be tempted to do so still. But the truth is that evangelisation is essential to any true and abiding reconstruction of life. The War has ended in a catastrophic vindication of the gospel of Jesus Christ. More lies broken on the field than Prussian militarism. Thus the world perceives that justice, mercy, truth and love are the necessary foundations of society. The Galilaean has conquered, and His Church is under constraint to proclaim Him as the one hope of the future. With the Apostle she cries aloud :

Vae enim mihi est si non evangelizavero.

November 30, 1918.

CONTENTS

I

INTRODUCTION

EVANGELISTIC ardour would seem to demand the enthusiasm of youth, and to belong to the beginnings of religious movements rather than to their maturity, to the first fervour of new spiritual experience rather than to so ancient, organised, and established an institution as the Church of England. Nevertheless there has recently appeared a very challenging document, emanating from a committee set up by the Archbishops to inquire into the evangelistic work of the Church, which boldly recommends a concentration of the whole attention of the Church " for a time with disproportionate attention " upon the evangelisation of England and the English people. This recommendation is pressed with the greatest urgency in the light of the religious situation which war has revealed. " Everywhere men are rising to higher levels of life, inspired by the call to service, self-discipline, and sacrifice ; inspired, that is to say, by an ideal of which the life of Christ is the supreme exhibition. Yet at the same time the majority of the people are without any conscious or explicit recognition of Christ as Saviour and King. All but a comparatively small minority of the nation are out of living touch with any form of institutional Christianity." [1]

I

There are some critics of this Report who, while admitting its statement of the situation, regard this call to the Church to concentrate upon its evangelistic duty as ill-timed. The preoccupation of war, the strain imposed upon

[1] *The Evangelistic Work of the Church*, S P.C.K., 1918, p. 30.

2

mind and time, the depletion of the ranks of the home clergy in response to the demands of National Service and of the spiritual needs of the Army, the absence of the younger men at the war, and the occupation of the younger women upon war service, may all be urged, they feel, as reasons against bringing forward any new evangelistic proposals at such a time as this. If what were contemplated by the Evangelistic Report were some vast preaching effort, such as that which marked the opening of the National Mission in the autumn of 1916, these might constitute valid arguments, but it is made perfectly clear that what is here recommended is far other and greater than any temporary effort of preaching. It is indeed nothing less than a revolution in the entire aim and direction of the thought and activities of the Church, the " radical re-education of our ecclesiastical thinking," so that the evangelistic duty of the Church, too long neglected and forgotten, may take its true place, dominating every department of its life and determining its policy and objective. " The evangelisation of England must pass from the margin to the centre of the mind of the Church. It is a question of right thinking." A " generous year " is named, but that year is to be spent not in some great effort to reach the unevangelised, but in compassing this change of outlook and aim in the Church herself. There is no need to wait for the end of war before attempting this. Right thinking is possible even with a depleted clergy, and once evangelisation dominates the consciousness of the Church there need be no fear but that, when opportunity offers, the great outward movement of evangelisation will begin.

It is hardly to be denied that in the past the consciousness of the Church has been predominantly pastoral in the narrower and exclusive sense which opposes pastoral and evangelistic. The

4

parochial system has carried such a suggestion. Lay folk and clergy alike have been more conscious of the parish priest's duty to the faithful who compose his congregation than to the souls within his cure committed to his charge. " To seek for Christ's sheep that are dispersed and for His children who are in the midst of this naughty world " is indeed insisted upon in the Ordinal as the standard of priestly duty, but in effect it must be confessed his other duty, " to feed and provide for the Lord's family," has had the pre-eminence. It is scarcely a matter of surprise that it should be so.

But there is new blood stirring in the English Church to-day, impatient of stagnation and routine. Now is the time in which she may hope to recover the evangelistic spirit. And indeed she cannot afford to wait. Reform, renewal, and reconstruction must engage her thought, and their first effect must be to restore her sense of proportion. Till the end of time the first duty of the Church will be evangelistic. Nor can this change of heart and mind be relegated till after the war without disaster. In every other department of life, from the Labour Party to the House of Lords, the necessity of change is recognised and is already at work. It is true that the most vigorous sons of the Church are away, but they are the most impatient for the Church at home to reform herself *without delay*. " The return of our armies to civil life," says the Report, " may be nearer or more distant than we anticipate, but it increases immeasurably the urgency of the evangelistic situation. When they come back from the tremendous experience of war they will be searching critics of the Church. They will look to find in it a brotherhood waiting to receive them into its fellowship, and a religious life which will bring them the succour that they need in a time of dangerous reaction. They will demand

6

reality of the Church."[1] The men are returning now. Four hundred thousand are already demobilised. Only by the recovery of the evangelistic spirit can the Church hope to give them the gospel of life in Christ which is their birthright, of which the noble spirit of self-sacrifice they have displayed has proved them to be worthy.

II

It will be evident to any reader of these pages that the writer believes that Catholicism alone has a gospel to offer adequate to the spiritual needs of this generation. That belief was strengthened by his experience of evangelistic work in New Zealand and Western Canada. The conditions into which the old world is now passing in many ways approximate to those of the new world. There life is characterised by the absence of convention and of the restraining influence of old associations

[1] Evangelistic Report, p. 31.

and long-established sanctions. Here in
the old world these are rapidly breaking
up, and their reign is already at an end.
The entry of America into the war and
the great part borne in it by the overseas Dominions, and the presence of
their stalwart soldiers here in the old
country *en route* for France, hastens the
process. Catholicism has three gifts to
offer to the new age which only the
prejudices of the old, now rapidly dying,
would disparage. Thus Catholicism
understands how to teach men to worship. It has discovered how to appeal
to the imagination and to surround the
approach to God with the suggestion
of mystery and wonder. It knows the
value of beauty in the presentation to
the mind of the sublimity of God. It
is strong on the side where Protestantism
and Puritanism were weak, and it is
a side of religion which is indispensable
to the modern world. Again, Catholicism is strong in the sense of the underlying spirituality of the visible world.

8

The sacramental system, reaching its climax in the Presence of Christ in the Blessed Sacrament, casts a halo over all common life, and breaks down the false and artificial barrier between the sacred and the secular which in part explains the failure of religion to make good its appeal to the spirit of an age that has learnt, from the diffused socialism which colours all its thought, to reject any religion which deals only with the invisible to the disregard of earth. This century is ready for a sacramental religion which will consecrate earthly elements as the channels of divine life; it cries aloud to discern God's presence in common things. And, further, Catholicism, in the value that it sets upon fellowship as a means of grace, appeals to the deepest instincts of our time. It offers men the first and only international society, a Catholic Church, which, whatever its failure hitherto to unite the nations and avert the disaster of war, is now seen to be not only a grand idea but a world necessity. Nor is it only the sense of union with Christ's men in every nation that Catholicism brings. It links us with the past, and carries us in its continuity to fellowship and union with the long evolution of Christ's Kingdom upon earth. We are one with all the ages, and know ourselves to be in the direct line of life with the slow but surely progressing impulse which dates from Pentecost. We make no doubt that the Society of Christ which abolished the arena, educated European civilisation, and taught mankind philanthropy, will finally make war impossible. To be of the Catholic Church is to be of the family of the Saints, who have been the true pioneers of humanity, and whose inspiration and influence still remain. Such a Catholicism constitutes an essentially modern appeal. But the experience which convinced me that it is essential to modern evangelisation convinced me no less that Catholicism itself is in need of restatement and re-presentation. It

can only communicate its gifts to the
new world upon the condition that it
is true to its largest self. It must shake
off all that has confined its universality
within national limits, and show itself
free of all alliances with the Caesarism
which has too largely influenced its past.
Catholicism in alliance with absolutism
can make no great appeal to the world
of to-day, even if that alliance be only
in the region of ideas. Liberty must
be seen, grown to equal stature with
authority, in the Catholicism which hopes
to bring the gospel of Christ to the nations
that lead the van of the world's progress.
My own faith is that, alike by its history
and its nature, the Church of England
is destined by God to be the main instrument in the bringing in of the largest
and the truest conception of Catholicism,
and, it may be, to be its first home.
Catholicism may be described as the
synthesis of the racial experience of God.
It holds within itself all that is noblest
in the spiritual history of Egypt, Israel,

Greece, and Rome. It is not inconceivable that the race which has been the mother of liberty in Europe, and is still its mainstay, may, through the Church which so remarkably reflects its national life, make its contribution to the fulness and perfection of Catholicism by the infusion of its own passion for freedom.

The Catholic movement in the Church of England is standing at the crossroads. Conscious of failure to carry the great mass of that communion to articulate and definite Catholicism, it now finds a new evangelistic opportunity opening before it. In the National Mission came the first signs of the change of mind for which Anglicanism is preparing. Two schools of counsel offer their advice. The "Ultramarines," as Mr. Ronald Knox cleverly named them, point to the efficiency of Roman methods. They call upon the Catholic party to adopt them wholesale. Benediction, exposition, rosary, and the like, they

12

suggest, have the attractive appeal which will command success, and the clear-cut precision of the Penny Catechism is the way to teach England the Catholic faith. They would seem insufficiently to have considered how deeply the political aspect of Roman Catholicism has affronted English religious feeling during the war. The Papal silence regarding German methods of warfare and the glaring misuse of ecclesiastical influence by the Irish Roman Catholic hierarchy have suggested to many, whose respect and admiration for many achievements of the illustrious Church of Rome had been ardent and sincere, that between absolutism in politics and in religion there is an unfortunate *liaison*. It is not wise to seek to commend Catholicism to England at this hour by approximation to the Roman style and outlook. Other counsellors desire to see the Catholic movement in England transformed by the infusion of the missionary spirit. It must, they con-

13

sider, change its detached and exclusive spirit; it must enter into and penetrate the corporate life of the Church of England.

It is useless to present the truths of religion to the England of our day upon the mere fiat of authority, " This is the Catholic faith, believe it or perish." Like the Apostle, we must be ready to give a reason for the faith that is in us. We shall best recommend our religion if we can show its value and necessity to life, that it offers to the intellect the highest revelation of truth, to the soul the deepest satisfaction of the religious instinct in devotion to the Person of Our Lord, and to the conscience the noblest ethical education in the imitation of His example and the application of His teaching to social, national, and international life. It must not be left to the non-Catholic world to take the lead in the application of Christian ethics to these problems. The Catholic Church has in the lives of its saints set

14

before the world a lofty and beautiful
standard of personal ethics. Its present
representatives are called to lead the
way in the development of the corporate
conscience. Catholicism must teach not
only the Christian verities but their
values, not only devotion but its ethics,
not only the doctrine of the Church but
its place in the forefront of human progress. Too long has it been content to
celebrate beautiful services to the joy
of eclectic congregations, but indifferent
or superior in its attitude to the " moderate " multitudes. These it must learn
to love if it is to win them. It must
gain a greater breadth and balance, a
charity which will diminish nothing of
the essential gift of Catholicism, yet
will hold cheap all personal satisfactions
in non-essentials in its burning eagerness
to open to an England, ready to receive
it, the sacred treasure of sacramental
life. Change there must be. Anglo-
Catholicism cannot live if it is to go on
in the old ruts. Its choice lies between

narrowness and breadth, between the passion for truth and the tolerance of superstition, between spiritual selfishness and evangelistic zeal, between freedom and autocratic authority, between loyalty to its own soul and the insinuating temptation to don the ill-fitting armour of its big Roman brother. Its evangelistic value depends upon the choice. Only in the name of evangelisation am I bold enough to appeal to those for whom, as for me, the Catholic ideal is the beautiful and the true, to consider afresh how it may best be presented to our countrymen with the hope of general acceptance. Has not the time come for the van to cry halt unless it is to be utterly severed from the main body? Anglo-Catholicism has everything to gain by a closer and more sympathetic contact with the rank and file of the Church of England, and by a freer interchange of thought and larger co-operation in work with moderates and evangelicals. It would receive bene-

16

fits as large as it would confer. In the foreign field the common task of evangelisation has drawn together into the most cordial relationships missionaries of divergent views, and at home evangelistic concentration may be expected to produce the same result.

But unless Anglicanism has some real part to play and contribution to make towards a broader and freer Catholicism than the Roman, what is its *raison d'être*, why cling to it any longer? However far it travel along the Roman road, judged by that standard of comparison it remains but a poor reproduction, neither international nor imperial. It cannot, while it plays the part of humble imitator, hope to rival even in its ceremonies the easy manners of "the old firm carrying on the old business in the old way." Still less can it aspire to be the religion of the English people, whose spiritual ideals move steadily and swiftly towards a Catholicism of breadth, freedom, and truth. The Catholic Church of the future will be no despotic Empire, but a communion of free Churches. The Church of England, whatever its faults, is the expression of the principle that it is possible for a Church to be national without being Protestant, and sacramental without a Pope. If it be true to itself, claiming life and liberty, and catholic to the core, it may be the *avant-courier* of the Church of the Apocalyptic vision, into which they shall bring the glory and honour of the nations.

II

THE PRIMARY DUTY OF THE CHURCH

THE Church, no less than the Nation, is looking forward with hope to the reconstruction which must follow the war. Already new possibilities of service are opening before her. Old conventions which had restricted her freedom of movement are disappearing. Old abuses, ignorances, and negligences which have rendered her impotent adequately to fulfil her divine mission in the world are threatened. The Church of England is conscious of the stirring within her of a new and vigorous, if impatient, youth. From within more than from without comes an insistent demand for liberty to live to the full her own spiritual life. It is therefore high time, upon the threshold of a new era of opportunity, to reconsider *ab initio* what is the service which the Church exists to render. " First things first " is the lesson of war-time.

Our Lord has Himself defined the primary duty of the Church in His final charge to the Apostles at His ascension. *Go ye therefore, and make disciples of all the nations, baptizing them into the name of the Father and of the Son and of the Holy Ghost : teaching them to observe all things whatsoever I commanded you : and lo, I am with you alway, even unto the end of the world* (St. Matt. xxviii. 19-20). St. Mark's version is equally definite. *Go ye into all the world, and evangelise every creature. He that believeth and is baptized shall be saved ; but he that believeth not shall be damned* (St. Mark xvi. 15-16). There would seem to be no room here for divergent views of the Church's chief duty. It is evangelisation.

20

Christian men would answer the question, What *is* the Church? in a hundred different ways. For our part we are well content with the Catholic and Pauline conception of the Church as Christ's Body upon earth, in which, by the grace of Pentecost, His Spirit is incarnate, the living organism in which He dispenses divine life to men by sacramental channels, wherein in an extended incarnation He still walks the earth in the visible fellowship of the redeemed, who, by the initiation of Baptism, are welded into a unity which the divisions of Christendom may conceal but cannot destroy. But in a descending scale a hundred different answers would diminish this conception till the point was reached where men see nothing more in the Church of Christ than a convenient association for working purposes of co-religionists who happen to be Christians. But, whatever our view of the nature of the Church, there is general agreement that its first

21

duty is to evangelise. Our Lord's evangelistic commission places that beyond dispute. It contains also His own interpretation of evangelisation. Its field the world, its process to make disciples, its content a gospel of life to be taught undiminished to all men, its method a fellowship, its motive power and inspiration the unfailing Presence of Christ Himself pledged and assured for all time. What more profitable exercise could there be in days like these, alike for the Church and the individual, than to test the aim of our activities by comparison with Christ's standard of the Church's duty ?

War has taught us the relationship of our individual lives not only to our nation but to mankind, as it becomes clearer that the issue of the war will affect for good or ill the whole future of humanity. It is less difficult for us nowadays to break loose from a narrowly individualistic and self-centred religion and to stretch our minds wide enough to take in the Church's burden as our own. That which is the first duty of the Church is the first duty of every member of it.

Evangelisation was inevitably the primary task of the Church at the beginning ; Jesus Christ was content to rest the whole future of Christianity upon the evangelistic spirit of His disciples. He was about to withdraw His visible presence. To what did He trust that the world, which as yet was in ignorance of all that had happened under Pilate in Jerusalem, should come to the knowledge of its redemption ? There was before Him the method which Mahomet chose—the book. He rejected it with a singular completeness. It is no disparagement of the credibility of the four Gospels which we possess, and the beauty of the portrait of our Lord which severally and in combination they present, if we allow imagination to ask what would the world give to-day for the autobiography of Jesus Christ,

23

or even for a report of His teaching
signed by Himself! But when Jesus
wrote He wrote in the dust of the Temple
court, and the feet of the first passers-
by obliterated His writing. Jesus put
His faith not in a book, but in living
men possessed by His Spirit : "*Go ye
. . . ye shall be My witnesses.*" Through
inspired and consecrated personality He
trusted to evangelise the world. If the
evangelistic spirit had burnt low in the
first disciples, and if the Church had
failed Him, what would the world to-day
have known of Jesus Christ ? Well-
nigh a quarter of a century passed
before a single book of the New Testament was in existence ; it was not complete till the close of the first century.
Only by a Church which recognised
evangelisation as its supreme duty could
the gospel have reached the outer world.

In a true sense this original necessity
recurs with every fresh generation, and
each generation creates a new evangelistic problem. " My son," said a modern

preacher, " is a lover of music, and so am I, but his music is not mine. He is all for the new composers. I stand by the classics. He hears music where I find discord and chaos. And his religion is as different from mine as his music. The letters he is sending home from France are full of things which he has found in the Bible that I never saw there." There is no crossing the gulf that separates the generations. We cannot look out upon life from the standpoint of our children. Nor is this inability altogether a matter for regret. The hope of the future lies in the capacity of each generation to see further than the last, and the recollection of our own youth ought to preserve us from nervous or grudging suspicions of the advance of the rising generation. But the father is conscious of a debt that he owes to his son. He must hand on to him the noble tradition of the past, verified and enlarged by his own experience of life. He cannot, nor need he desire to save

25

his son the necessity laid upon us all of buying our experience by the things which we suffer, but his warnings and counsels, and, above all, his personal influence and example, will leave upon him an indelible impression, and largely contribute to the final determination of character and faith that makes the man. Our theories, predilections, and prejudices die with us, but we may, if we will, communicate to those who follow us the kernel of our spiritual experience. " Where did your son get his religion from ? " the father quoted above was asked. He answered grandly, " From his mother and me."

It may be left to the curious to conjecture what would be the fate of Christianity in the world did any generation utterly fail in this evangelistic duty which it owes to its successor. No generation has so failed, but they have not been equally successful, and the ebb and flow of the power of Christianity in the world has been the direct consequence of this variation. It may be that the New Testament is now sufficient security for the permanence of Christianity, but with the spectacle of Germany before our eyes, it is evident that it could not remain the master-force in history unless the Church retained through the centuries the freshness and zeal of its evangelistic spirit.

III

THE NEW EVANGELISM

THE Evangelistic Report contains a definition of evangelisation: "*To evangelise is so to present Jesus Christ in the power of the Holy Spirit that men may come to put their trust in God through Him, to accept Him as their Saviour, and to serve Him as their King in the fellowship of His Church.*"

No member of the Committee which produced the Report would, perhaps, so have defined it at the outset; some comment, therefore, on its significance may be permitted. Evangelisation is here defined in the first instance as a certain "presentation of Jesus Christ." How he will present his subject is the care of every wise teacher. He is not content

28

to memorise text-books. He finds himself equally concerned in the study of the personality of his pupils. He must know their need and capacity, be of quick and sympathetic insight, able to place his own mind side by side with theirs, so that by the play of mind on mind he may find the right approach. The evangelist also, in so far as he is a teacher, works under the same conditions, nor can he content himself with the study of the individual only, apart from his generation. Every great evangelistic movement has set Christ before men in a new light according to the special needs and habits of thought of the time, though in all ages the essential Evangel has been the same, for it has been the Christ Himself. The gospel is more than a philosophy of life, more than a new and loftier ethic, more than a romantic history of a divine life once lived upon earth. None of these would alone be sufficient to evangelise men. It is the Personality of Jesus Christ now

29

alive upon earth, discernible in the life of those whom He calls His witnesses, and pre-eminently in the corporate life of the Christian fellowship. "In the power of the Holy Spirit" runs the definition. *Lo, I am with you alway*, said the ascending Christ, but He bade them await the descent of the Spirit. Evangelisation must tarry for Pentecost. The indwelling Spirit of Christ in His Church is the first essential of all evangelisation. We are here warned against putting our trust in organisation. We may plan evangelistic campaigns and carry them through with zeal and energy, and yet fail to evangelise. American evangelists have created new notions of the place of advertisement in evangelisation, and there are those among us who desire to see the Church institute a campaign of publicity which would imitate the methods employed to stimulate recruiting at the beginning of war, and placard on every hoarding the appeal of Christ. Such methods are singularly unlike those of our Lord Himself. He appears to have avoided the crowds and to have shrunk from publicity. Thus it was His habit to caution those whom He healed not to spread abroad the tale of His miracles. But without condemning a reasonable use of the printing press, the supreme need, and the only necessity, is the Spirit of Christ seen in individual and corporate life, which is itself the witness to His Presence and the evidence of His Power. Where the Spirit is, there the gospel is always being spread. Like the *élan vital* of which the French philosopher speaks, the Holy Spirit in the Church of Christ and in the Christian man is a life-impulse, continually pressing onwards and outwards. A new reliance upon the Holy Spirit, a new desire of His Presence, and surrender to His Will is still the source of all evangelistic victory, as it has been in Christian history the hidden spring of every evangelistic movement of revival. Only by being filled with His Presence and His

31

Spirit can we present Christ to the world. Historic imagination is at work seeking to bring Him to life in the old pages of the gospel, and vividly to set Him before men as He was—a noble service to evangelisation, but it is not enough. Art, more perfectly in the past than now, has made its own beautiful contribution to the Evangel. Poetry has sung its lyrics of the love of Jesus, but neither the rhyme of St. Bernard nor the art of Italy are sufficient to evangelise. The Spirit of Christ still living in His servants is the sole evangelist.

But life lived in Christ must confess its secret and its Master. Always a silent witness it may not always remain silent. Witness that is permanently inarticulate will produce no disciples. The reserve of an Englishman's religion may have in it fine elements of sincerity and reverence, yet it may often spring from moral cowardice. It is largely because we have allowed our Christian witness to be over-silent that the religion of our generation is so vague and inarticulate. Why should we disguise our discipleship or submit to the convention that excludes the direct acknowledgement of Christ as our Master from ordinary conversation ?

The evangelist seeks to present Christ to men *so that they may come to put their trust in God through Him.* He brings to them Christ's presentation of God. As we study our Lord's evangelistic method we discover that His one concern was to change men's thought of God. In the minds of His hearers there was indeed a lofty conception of Deity. They thought of God as the one, infinite, holy Spirit ; but in this sublime conception of God His righteousness was the dominant thought. He was the God of Sinai ; thunder and lightning were His symbols ; rigid and exact to enforce the law written on tables of stone ; remote and unapproachable, a God to dread rather than to trust. " Only believe the good news of God," was Christ's evangelistic appeal. St. Luke's fifteenth chapter, which con-

33 D

tains our Lord's defence of His evangelistic method against the criticisms of the
representatives of the traditional Jewish
idea of God, gives us without doubt His
way of bringing the "publicans and
sinners" of His day to a new vision of
God, which would build up in them both
hope and trust. He taught them to
think of God as of a good shepherd who
would go after a strayed sheep till He
found it; or a woman who could not
rest till she had recovered a coin lost
from her dower-necklace—the wedding-
ring in its modern equivalent—as a
father yearning for the return of the
son who had left him. This is a picture
of God which could not but burst on His
Jewish hearers with the force of a new
revelation. It must have struck at the
roots of despair. Hope and faith are
the most essential factors in the transformation of consciousness by which
life, ruined by follies and sins, can alone
be restored. What an image of God
was this for such a purpose—as pitiful

34

and understanding as the shepherd, as persistent as a woman in His search for His lost treasure, as wise and patient, as generous and forgiving as the father of the heedless lad. Is there in all literature such largeness of love packed into a sentence?—*While he was yet a great way off his father saw him, and ran to meet him, and fell on his neck and kissed him again and again.* Yet what strength there was in this father. Not a word to hold back the lad from the experience of life in which man is made and remade. He gives him full portion the moment he asks it. It is the prerogative of freedom to learn by what we suffer. God does not deal with a son as with a sheep.

Our evangelistic problem in these war days is how to preserve men's trust in God. The colossal suffering and ruin which war is inflicting have roused in innumerable minds questionings which go to the very roots of the idea of God. How can a good God tolerate such

abomination ? Why does He not inter-
vene to end the war ? Why does He
not smite down the guilty nation ? Is
it love or strength He lacks ? The
answer is to be found in Christ's presentation of God.

His sons have got to be free;
Their wills are their own and their lives are their
    own,
And that's how it has to be.[1]

A God content to let men in nations
learn in the school of history the worth
and glory of right choice, and that

It's wiser being good than bad;
    It's safer being meek than fierce;
It's fitter being sane than mad.

Only on the basis of Christ's conception of God can any man say :

My own hope is a sun will pierce
The thickest cloud earth ever stretched;
    That after Last, returns the First,
Though a wide compass round be fetched :
    That what began best, can't end worst,
Nor what God blessed once, prove accurst.

But this strength of God which does
not withdraw His sons from the most

[1] *Rough Rhymes of a Padre*, Studdert Kennedy.

36

bitter experience of suffering and evil is no failure but rather the climax of His love. Seen in the long views of God, the sufferings which end in such relations of love between God and His world, as those which our Lord describes between father and son at the feast which celebrated their reunion, may well appear worth while. A world that has freely chosen the will of God for its international law, and the Kingdom of Heaven as the basis of its civilisation, given an eternity into which man's earthly achievement will reach forward into unimaginable glory, is worth the sacrifice of blood.

God, as Christ conceived Him, is a God to be trusted even in a world-war, and evangelisation is the right name for all efforts which seek so to present Christ to men that they shall come to put their trust in God through Him.

To accept Him as their Saviour is the old familiar language of the gospel. It enshrines the central evangelical experience of the soul in its conversion—

awakening, pardon, peace, and a new and transformed life springing out of the personal discovery of Jesus. It is to be feared that this definite experience was more frequent in the last generation. It rested on a more vivid personal sense of sin than is common to-day. War by its revelation of the destructive power of evil may be expected to arrest the decay of the sense of sin, and with the longing for release from its inner bondage will return again the old recognition of Jesus the Saviour. But we may expect that this name of Christ will bear a broader connotation.

Salvation was regarded in the past as an all but exclusively individual affair : " God and my soul, my soul and God." But there is springing up the wider vision of a World-Saviour, who will not only gather into His Kingdom the millions of individual souls, but will bring to an earth, ready at last to accept Him as its Deliverer, national and international " salvation."

When Mary named her son " Jesus " at the bidding of the angel, she gave Him a name which had for Jewish ears the suggestion that Napoleon carries for the French, or Wellington and Nelson for ourselves. Jesus, or Joshua, was the name of the national hero who had led the race, escaped from its Egyptian slavery, to victory and liberty, to sovereignty in a land of promise. *He shall save his people from their sins* is no mere promise of individual deliverance from the inner slavery of the mind to the lower nature. The coming of Christ to the soul is indeed this personal salvation. Mind and spirit in Him find their sovereignty and freedom of self-determination. But to save His *people* means race-freedom from race-sin, and world-freedom from world-sin. As the war has gone on it has become increasingly clear that the real issue is between the acceptance or the rejection of Jesus Christ as World-Saviour, and His *Weltpolitik* of love as the basis of international law.

To serve Him as their King is included in the definition of the new evangelism, and together with the words which follow, " in the fellowship of His Church," constitutes its most original element. It is the direct result of the study of the soul of our own generation. Later in these pages the essential Christianity of the ideal of service is insisted on, as also its present wide appeal. It is here included as an essential part of the evangelistic message because the " christening " of service is the true work of an evangelistic Church. The gospel is no mere presentation in the name of religion of ideals popular at the moment, but their uplifting to definite spiritual value by their consecration to the name of Christ. There are many who would say that it is a matter of small moment whether or no service be consecrated to Christ. He will accept it at full value, even if it be not consciously done in His name, and they would quote St. Matthew: " Inasmuch

as ye have done it unto one of the least of
these My brethren ye have done it unto
Me." But the evangelist cannot rest
content with unconscious and inarticulate service of Christ. During the South
African War, near the end of her life,
Queen Victoria visited the wards at
Netley Hospital. Her chair was wheeled
to the bedside of one poor fellow who
lay grievously broken. She thanked
him with tears : " It was for me that
you suffered this." Seeing his Queen,
and receiving from her own lips this
grateful recognition, the soldier could
hardly fail to discover a new honour in
his wounds that would ease his pain and
ennoble his sacrifice. It could not fail
to strengthen him to face the burden
which his injuries would impose upon
his future. Patriotism, touched by
personality, would be transfigured by
the word which gave to his sufferings
the character of devotion to his
Queen. To pass from inarticulate
Christianity to the personal discovery

41

of Jesus Christ in the life of service is infinitely more ennobling and inspiring. This is the contribution which the wider conception of evangelism has to offer. The true service of man is always the service of Christ, but only they who see the Christ they serve draw from their service the full power that is in it to consecrate life afresh. They only are, in the Gospel phrase, " made whole," for they have found in Christ that which unites life in one single purpose, communicating to all its activities a new strength, endurance, and delight. Men whose daily service is done in the name of liberty deserve to find in Christ a King whose service is perfect freedom.

The climax of the new definition of evangelisation " *in the fellowship of His Church* " belongs equally to its original conception and our modern needs. Evangelisation is imperfectly understood when it is regarded mainly from the point of view of personal salvation.

Fellowship, brotherhood, and unity were predominant in the mind of Christ. Even in His teaching about prayer, fellowship holds a high place. It was, He taught, the secret of its power, and the means of His own Presence with them as they prayed. Where two or three were gathered in His name, unanimous in their desire, they were to be assured of His presence and of the answer to their petition. The Lord's Prayer is indeed a protest against individualistic religion. Fellowship was His method of attaining the desire of His heart, the coming of the Kingdom of Heaven upon earth. Only by a society could society be redeemed, only by a kingdom could the Kingdom come. It would be as true to say that He saw in every man of good-will a possible soldier and servant of His Church as to say that He created a Church for the supply of his soul's necessities. The Sacraments are the standing witness that to Christ the fellowship of man with man is the royal

43

road to union with God. Every one of
the Sacraments is an act of fellowship.
It is but the barest truth, therefore, to
affirm that no man is evangelised who
has not found his place in the historic
fellowship which Christ set up upon
earth. No gospel which offers men a
private religion of personal relationship
to Jesus but leaves them unrelated to
Christ's Body upon earth is the authentic
Christian gospel. The Christian call to
service is an even larger call than the
philanthropic self-devotion to the welfare
of others. It is the call to the definite
service of the Kingdom of Christ. More
is asked of the Christian man than that
by the grace of God he should do his
duty in that state of life to which he is
called. His baptism enlists him in the
Christian crusade, and unites him to the
millions who have seen the vision of a
new heaven and a new earth and live
for its realisation.

IV

THE COMPLETE DISCIPLE

THE definition of evangelisation which I have endeavoured to interpret might be regarded with some suspicion unless it could be shown that it truly expresses the purpose of our Lord's original evangelistic commission to His Church. In fact it is implicit in His words. *Go ye into all the world and make disciples* is nothing else than the command so to present Him to men that they may come to put their trust in God through Him. To accept Him as Saviour and serve Him as King is clearly nothing else than to be a disciple, while to baptize is to complete discipleship by admission to the Fellowship.

45

I

A disciple is a learner, yet he is no mere student. The disciple implies the master through whom he derives his knowledge. He is more than a pupil, he is an adherent. Loyalty as well as intelligence goes to the making of the good disciple. Discipleship is a personal relationship. The good disciple reflects his master. So men appraised Christ's disciples. *They took knowledge of them that they had been with Jesus.* The stamp of His personality was apparent on them. It is no light task that is laid upon the Church, to make men disciples of an invisible Master. How is the intimate personal knowledge of Christ which is the mark of the disciple to be communicated at second-hand ? It would indeed be impossible but for His mystical presence in the Church and in the soul. The Church which is His Body exists to make disciples to the Lord Christ by exhibiting the signs of

46

His power and presence. It is a mighty school of the personal knowledge of Jesus. There can be little doubt, having regard to the religious condition of England, that there rests upon the Church at this time the urgent duty of evangelisation in this sense of the word, disciple-making. The land is full of the Christian spirit. Heroism and self-sacrifice are eminently Christian virtues though they are not peculiar to Christendom. But neither is Christ, for with St. John we see in Christ the very soul of humanity. *He was in the world but the world knew Him not.* The lamp of sacrifice, wherever it shines, is the sign of His presence, unrecognised and unknown though it be. The jet of water leaping from the barren ground which has been pierced by an artesian boring betrays its origin on the slopes of unseen and distant hills. Similarly, war has penetrated the dry surface of common life, and has revealed, in unexpected profusion, instincts for self-sacrifice which defy the hereditary im-

47

pulse of self-preservation bred into the race by the struggle for existence. Here is discovered the evidence of the light that lighteth every man that cometh into the world, be it in the noble heathen of Sparta, Carthage, or Japan, in the heroism which inspires many a deluded soldier of Germany, or in the inarticulate devotion to the Christian ideal of life which animates the vast majority of our own countrymen in these days of trial.

" Myriads of souls were born again to ideas of service and sacrifice in those tremendous days," writes Mr. Wells. " Black and evil thing as war was it was at any rate a great thing. It did this much for countless minds that for the first time they realised the epic quality of history, and their own relationship to the destinies of their race. The flimsy roof under which we had been living our lives of comedy fell, and shattered the floor beneath our feet. We saw the stars above and the abyss below."

This is beyond question a just esti-mate of the effect of war stimulus upon multitudes who in time of peace were content to drift quietly through life without purpose or struggle. If to the words service and sacrifice be added discipline, an equally true and more complete description would be given of the advance to higher levels of life which the strain and challenge of our time have evoked. It is true that as yet we see no sign of any large return to conscious Christian discipleship. Christ is not, so far as we may judge, more widely confessed as Saviour or recognised as King, but nevertheless the spirit which He taught and exhibited has become the national ideal. Discipline, service, and sacrifice are words which well describe the earth-life of Jesus. They constitute, in fact, His biography in brief. The life at Nazareth was pre-eminently the period of His self-discipline; in its long restraint He learnt that mastery of self which is the secret of power. The three years of the public ministry were as conspicuously years of service in which the manual labourer of Nazareth turned

E

to minister to man's higher needs of bodily health, of intellectual illumination, and of spiritual union with the Father. The climax of His life of self-giving came in that death which has become for the world the summit of sacrifice. The life of discipline, service, and sacrifice is the Christian life, and it is being lived in these days of war in England by myriads who have never lived it before, but it is not for the sake of Jesus Christ, nor as His disciples, that they so live. Attracted by and already obedient to an ideal of life which is essentially Christian, they do not know the Christ, nor recognise Him in that ideal.

" They have never seen Him, that is the fact," writes a Chaplain in France in *As Tommy sees Us*, " have never seen the Jesus whose life is never sombre, who was possessed of a marvellous attractiveness for just such men as these, who never withdrew Himself from ordinary society, however vexed, who was never censorious but practised a catholic charity, who was not demonstrative or gushing, but had the dignity of a strong man, whose life was not narrow, but free and glad, who was not effeminate, but had in Him the constraining force of a great personality, who had a full, robust, male humanity : Him they have never seen. Our preaching and our corporate living have not availed to set Him before them."

Here is revealed a great need of Christian teaching, for without teaching the real Jesus Christ cannot be known, but it must be the teaching of those who themselves know Him whom they would make known to others with the disciple's knowledge of his Master. There is urgent need here in England of definite teaching about God and Christ, about the Church and the Sacraments, but it is the teacher that counts in any teaching, and pre-eminently in Christian teaching : book knowledge cannot save the world, nor a new edition of the Catechism deliver us from ignorance of Jesus Christ. The old Catechism was grandly based, despite its admitted gaps,[1]

---

[1] *E.g.* the Catechism contains no statement of the unity of God, and may thus be in part responsible for much of the prevalent tritheism.

and despite a feudal phrase or two. It
is noble in its insistence upon duty, and
psychologically sound in its scheme of
Christian teaching : first the faith, then
duty, then the grace of prayer and
sacraments. But when we have revised
the Catechism, we have not provided
for that need which led Jesus Christ to
put His trust not in evangels but in
evangelists. The communication of the
saving knowledge of Christ is from life
to life, and it is so because those who
have found Jesus Christ are by that
Lord indwelt, and as they surrender
themselves to His life become the expression and manifestation of the living
Christ here upon earth. And the Church
so indwelt in the fulness of her corporate
life exists to be the expression of His
perfection, the revelation of the fulness
of Him who filleth all in all. That she
be possessed by the Christ is the first
quality which will make her His true
Evangelist.

It is not in one rank of society alone

that discovery of the living Christ is needed. English gentlemen who come from our public schools, and those upon whom rests the supremely evangelistic task of teaching them religion, no less than democracy struggling into the consciousness of its life and power, and those who in whatever capacity are honoured to serve them, share one common need : it is the revelation of Christ, the manifestation of the Master, the discovery of the living Jesus, as the source of those high ideals for the uplift of human life which fire so many in our age with the enthusiasm of a religion. To one and all alike he only who knows the Lord Christ can communicate the knowledge of Him. St. Paul is our encouragement. Alone of all the great New Testament figures he, it would appear, had not seen Christ in the flesh, yet St. John himself scarcely surpasses St. Paul's understanding and experience of the mind and heart of Jesus Christ. In page after page of his glowing letters

we discover his intimate knowledge of
his invisible Lord. He had learnt Christ,
as we may learn Him, in the secret
communion of his prayer, and in the
daily experience of life lived in His
Presence. Possessed by His life Paul
was His supreme evangelist to the Gentile
world. The root of discipleship was in
him : *To me to live is Christ. Not I,
but Christ that liveth in me.* Yet mark
what brought St. Paul to his discovery.
He who was to write the first word of
the New Testament had no New Testament from which to learn Christ. He
learnt Him through a life—through a
life which was a glorious death. Paul
watched the dying Stephen, and he
beheld in the martyr a new spirit, the
Christ-spirit. As Stephen prayed for
his murderers while the stones fell upon
him he exhibited not only a new moral
splendour, but the presence of Christ
in him. This was the root of Paul's
discovery of Jesus, from which sprang
the power of the vision upon the road

54

to Damascus to produce his " wonderful conversion." It is not only the duty of the Church of Christ to exhibit Jesus Christ, it is the bounden duty of every single member of it so to live that Christ may be seen in him.

II

And to be a disciple is to be of a fellowship. A common loyalty unites all who are disciples of the same Master. Evangelisation has not done its work until it has brought men into the fellowship. That is the significance of the baptismal covenant : *Baptizing them into the Name of the Father, and of the Son, and of the Holy Ghost.* Baptismal regeneration is no dull old dry-as-dust dogma of mechanical sacramentalism, no theological battle-axe wherewith to brain a heretic, no blind attribution of impossible spiritual experience to babes, it is the grand affirmation of the democratic faith that human fellowship is a sacrament of divine life ;

that to receive a child into that divine society, which Christ founded upon earth to be the perfect expression of the brotherhood of man and the ideal recognition of the all-Fatherhood of God, is to set him in the environment of an eternal and spiritual life. Baptism brings men into the fellowship, it links them to one another as it links them to Christ, and in the fellowship of His mystical body His presence is revealed. And if the world cannot discover Christ in His Church, is it not because the Church is deficient in fellowship, because she is herself torn and divided, because she has become exclusive rather than inclusive, because she has lost the great bond of universal charity and love which is the mark of the true catholicity, the catholicity not only of the creed but of the heart? We shall not convince the world that Jesus Christ lives in His Church, nor make disciples of our generation, till the Church herself exhibits His Spirit. *By this shall all men know that*

*ye are My disciples, if ye have love one
to another.*

There is no greater hindrance to
evangelisation than the divisions of
Christianity, and in no direction more
than in the " will to reunion," which is
to be seen gaining strength on all sides,
may we look forward with confidence to
the future. It would appear that as we
have learnt the folly of those efforts
towards unity which depended upon the
liberal sacrifice of principle and conviction—the undenominationalism which
was the bane of the nineteenth century—
there has been born into our hearts the
desire for a closer knowledge of the
thought and spiritual experience of those
who are separated from us denomination-
ally. It is not too much to say that
already sympathy and respect have taken
the place of the suspicion and contempt
which so long characterised the relation
of " the Churches " of baptized Christians. Already it has been found possible for the present writer to expound

and lead the devotion of the Fellowship
of Silence alternately in a Congregational
and an Anglican Church with episcopal
knowledge and approval.   One who describes himself as still a strong nonconformist, and formerly " guilty of a
strong and at times almost a bitter
spirit against the Church of England,"
writes of these meetings of silent fellowship :   " We must learn to worship
together first, then we may increase our
ways of working together.   At conferences and councils of clergy and ministers
you may get to know each other and
your points of view, but only in worship,
it seems to me, will you really get anything done that will fuse."

In the crypt of St. Paul's Cathedral,
in the presence of the Bishop, the
Moderator of the General Assembly of
the Church of Scotland recently declared
the readiness of many in his Church to
receive again episcopal succession, under
conditions which would at once respect
the conviction of the Churches that

regard episcopacy as essential to sacramental validity, and at the same time require of no man in presbyterian orders that he should deny his own past ministry, or go back upon his own spiritual experience and lineage.

This is indeed a sign of the times. The Moderator proved himself, it may be hoped, if no pontiff, a notable bridge-builder. The recognition that in the days of our separation God has not forsaken His people, but has given to them in their isolation a variety of experience which they may in His own way and time bring in to enrich the common heritage, is itself a stride forward towards the visible unity of the Church.

But if the Church can show to the world that she is filled with the spirit of fellowship, and exhibit in her life the presence of the Christ, there is waiting for her the welcome that is given to all evangelists who bring men the good news for which they are hungering.

The age is asking for Christ, and for fellowship. It needs but the touch of the Spirit of God, and an England that is prepared through the discipline of war may yet attain conscious devotion and discipleship to Jesus Christ. That is our task; it must be the primary concern of our own and of the Church's life. There was a picture in the Academy two or three years ago which all recognised upon the instant. It was of an explorer in the Antarctic stumbling in darkness and blizzard to his death; a light issued dimly from the tent he had left, the only relief in a terrible world of storm, darkness, and cold. That his comrades might have some faint chance of life he was forsaking their company, for which his heart hungered, as he sacrificed its solace rising to the heights of fellowship. Long after, when the relief party found the tent, but found not the body of him who left it, they built a cairn of ice and inscribed there : " Near to this place died a very

gallant gentleman." It was character-
istically English to write thus; English
in its reticence and reserve, English in
its fine perception that to be a gentleman
was to be willing to die for one's friends.
Yet, had it stopped at that, we should
have to add, English also in its in-
articulateness. But it did not stop there.
They wrote these words upon a cross
surmounting the ice cairn. In that
cross, though their lips did not frame the
word Christ, yet consciously or unconsciously they confessed what was
the source of all that was noble, beautiful, and true in the content of the words
" English gentleman."

I see there a symbol of the Church's
present task. It is ours to set the cross
above the cairn; to crown all noble
life and sacrificial death by the revelation of the Christ who is its spring, its
inspiration and reward.

V

THE WAR-PLOUGH

THE evangelistic situation is grave, but it is not depressing. I would even venture to affirm that the world-war has brought to the Church an evangelistic opportunity without parallel in its history. If stillness and peace favour the growth of the soul, storm, stress, and catastrophe often accompany and accomplish its regeneration. War has gone like a plough over the mind of this generation, cutting deep furrows into which an evangelistic Church may cast its seed with better hope of harvest than the smooth green fields of peace or the hard worn surface of familiar routine ever offered.

I

The war has brought back to the world the longing for deliverance from evil. How could the Church evangelise a world that had lost the sense of sin ? To announce a saviour, a deliverer, a redeemer, is no good news to men that sit at ease dreaming themselves secure, to men who imagine that under the genial and progressive influence of education and culture the lingering traces of the ape and the tiger, the last remains of barbarism in the blood, are rapidly vanishing and may be trusted shortly to disappear. Men who are not worrying about their sins do not feel the need of a Saviour. Even the Christian moralities were becoming to some but conventions destined to be superseded by a humanity beyond the old conflict of good and evil. What chance for evangelisation in such an atmosphere as that ? But the thunder of war has rudely disturbed these dreamers. The madness of Germany has taught the world again that evil is evil. However philosophers might disguise the insanity which ignores the difference between good and evil, translated into the grim reality of action it was unmistakable. The world watched in horror and amazement as Germany set herself to wage war upon every morality in an intellectual barbarity which no savage ever approached ; and it knows again that evil is of the devil and good is of God. The hour has come for an evangel that can offer to the world, to nations not less than to individuals, deliverance from the tyranny of evil through Jesus Christ the Redeemer.

Again, the heart of the evangel is the Cross, but when men are well-comforted and in peace, what need know they of the Cross ? To them it is no magnet, it is folly, it is a stumbling-block. Sorrow turns men to the Crucified. As the cruelty of war piles up the load of human suffering the world's necessity increases for such a God as is revealed in Christ.

It is God upon the Cross that men are crying out for now, men in millions who do not reason out their need, but in inarticulate pain stretch out their hands to the Infinite for help. This is the hour for the evangel of the Cross. In days like these " only the Infinite pity is sufficient for the Infinite pathos of human life." But the Cross is more than pity. It is the courage of God.

" The true God," writes Mr. Wells, " goes through the world with pipes and drums and flags calling for recruits along the street. We must go out to Him ; we must accept His discipline and fight His battle."

Great words ; and this is the first meaning of the Cross. Upon the Cross I see no effeminate and feeble Christ, no ancient of days, no sick and broken man, but One who in the full flower of His perfect manhood goes out to meet and conquer death in a sublime and solitary fortitude, alone against the world, sentenced by His Church, condemned by His nation, executed by the dominant

F

world power, forsaken even by His friends. There is no such symbol of courage in the world as the crucifix. To-day the attractive power of the Cross returns.

Yet again, war has done service to the evangel in that it has broken down two barriers which have held back the triumph of the Gospel in countless lives, narrowness of vision and self-centred preoccupation. Not long ago I visited the village of my boyhood. In the church hung proudly the long list of men on service, sons of the men whom their names recalled to my memory. " This one," said the vicar, " is in France, this in Palestine, this in Egypt." To the houses that lay nestling round the village-green letters were coming from the ends of the earth, and lines of communication centred there bearing to and fro the contact of love and prayer. The village had expanded both in heart and mind. There is not a village in the land, no sleepy hollow, no lonely hamlet, but has shared this opening of interest and vision. The war has redeemed life from pettiness and triviality. These wide horizons prepare the way for the Gospel. Even death itself is enlisted as an evangelist; for every name upon our roll of honour there are eyes that strain their sight beyond the farthest horizons to the far eternal whither he who bore that name has passed beyond our sight. Our generation is grown acutely conscious of God; God is named, discussed, and thought of far more to-day than four years ago. Books about God and prayer pour from the press and are eagerly bought. The ploughman's eyes are no longer fixed upon the furrow, nor the clerk's upon his ledger. Better that men should ask, " Why does not God stop the war ? " even though they do not find an answer, than that they should forget that there is a God in the triviality of common life. " My parish," said the parson in the oft-told tale, " wants an earthquake, not a quiet day." It has come. This is a great evangelistic opportunity; let but the Church rise to its chance, put away all lesser preoccupations that distract its interest, catch again the passion of the love of Christ, and, on fire with evangelistic zeal, go out to gather in the multitudes, and the Church may once again make history.

II

But the war is in its fifth year, the National Mission, though it is not yet finished with, as the appearance of the Reports of the five Committees of Inquiry remind us, has delivered its message, and yet the converts do not come.

"Ours is the golden age of evangelistic opportunity," says the Report of the Evangelistic Committee, "yet in fact it is a time of evangelistic impotence. So far from gaining new converts to our Lord, organised Christianity is found to be shrinking."

These are grave words, and the graver because they represent not merely the opinion of the individual members of the

Committee, but a mass of evidence received from all parts of England. That evidence receives strong confirmation from the Chaplains to the Forces. They have earned an irresistible right to our attention. I quote from *The Church in the Furnace* :

"He is no true lover of Christ and His Church who whines when he hears men speak of the Church's failure. It is too far-reaching to be lightly glossed over. One could wish every comfortable optimist in the Church at home had to pass through three months' experience with a brigade at the Front."

And again :

"Why are the vast majority of men who compose our armies almost completely unconscious of any sense of relationship with the Church of their Baptism? Why is the religion of most soldiers so largely inarticulate that they fail to connect the good things they do believe and practise with Jesus Christ?"

Hear another padre :

"Now one feels bound to say quite brutally that if the Church of England is in the future what it was before the war, we have lost these men for Christ irrevocably."

Those are strong words. What need we any further witness ? Yet ask the chaplains in the home camps how many men attend the voluntary services, how many receive Holy Communion. Or look round about our churches. The *Daily News* census of church-going in 1903 revealed the fact that in South London only one man in twelve went to any church on Sundays, and in the fifteen years that have elapsed since then church-going has still further declined. Church-going is, of course, no test of Christianity, but it is a very fair test of consciously Christian discipleship and of the value that a man sets upon his place in the Christian fellowship. He can hardly reckon himself a disciple of Jesus Christ and an adherent of His Fellowship if he habitually absents himself from the common Christian worship. In the towns parochialism is broken down. We have put congregationalism in its place. Here and there may be found a living centre gathered round a powerful personality,

some pulpit Chrysostom, it may be, or a
highly specialised and splendid worship
with every Catholic comfort and en-
trancing music. Here and there *esprit
de congrégation*; but the passion to
evangelise, to claim the splendid manhood of our race for a conscious devotion
to our Lord? England for Christ!—how
many of our congregations burn with
that fire? Truth to tell, it is seldom
even upon the margin of their consciousness. It may be true that church-going
in the past was often but a formal and
conventional affair, and that to-day it
represents more definite religious purpose, but we cannot be content to allow
any such comparisons to lull us into
comfortable satisfaction with the present.
Nor can we excuse ourselves by the
word of Christ, *few there be that enter
therein*, until we have satisfied ourselves
that we on our part have done all that it
is possible to do to clear away stumbling blocks and present Christ to His
people. The parochial system, even

though it be no arrogant claim to an exclusive evangelistic mission, is a frank and full acknowledgement of our responsibility for every living soul in England that, one way or another, it shall have the chance to come to the fulness of Christian discipleship.

VI

RIVAL EVANGELS

WAR, even if it has broken down some of the barriers that stood in the way of evangelisation, has laid bare an evangelistic situation that is alarming in its gravity; but it did not create that situation. Let us glance at the causes which led to the present condition of religion in England. Antecedents are not always depressing, and here we may discover elements in the present situation for which the Church is not wholly to blame. The years before the war were years of increasing difficulty for evangelisation. They witnessed the coming to maturity of the results of the Education Act of 1870 which gave England universal popular education.

They witnessed also the birth of halfpenny journalism. The preacher of to-
day finds himself with a racier, cheaper,
briefer rival, in the evening paper which
a man can read over his pipe by his own
fireside. The fictitious authority that
used to surround the pulpit has given
place to a no less fictitious infallibility
of print. A confusing, daring, sensa-
tional channel of ideas for the thinly-
educated reader, this same halfpenny
Press! The same years saw the thaw
and break up of many rigid conventions. Old habits disappeared—church-
going, Sunday-keeping, formal religious
observance among them — even the
moral standards and sanction of Christianity lost for many their axiomatic
authority in the period of transition
which preceded the war. Meanwhile a
vigorous rationalistic campaign, pressed
sometimes with eloquence and ready
wit, and making hostile use of the
more negative and destructive results
of Biblical criticism, sowed broadcast

the seeds of intellectual doubt and confusion.

The air was full of new movements which claimed men's support with an almost religious appeal by their gospels of humanity and their attractive programmes for the uplift of the conditions under which the masses were living. The Labour Movement offered to the industrial workers more than the satisfaction of class ambition and the removal of the disabilities and injustices under which too long they had chafed. The gospel of freedom, justice, and equal opportunity might claim, even more boldly than it has yet done, to be nothing else than Christianity in action. For the women a like conviction and attraction lay behind the appeal of the feminist movement. Here were two evangelistic rivals of the Church making a bid for that enthusiasm for humanity which is among the noblest endowments of man, evangelistic rivals out to make converts, I do not say to Christ, but to applied

Christianity. The same years saw also the rise into popularity of three movements which claimed definite spirituality, and in large measure exhibited it, each of which has made converts by the thousand. Christian Science has now its disciples all over the country and in every class. Spiritualism before the war, and even more since, is spreading with amazing rapidity. Theosophy has been only less successful in making disciples for its occult teaching, and in enlisting them into a brotherhood which offers itself as a world-wide fellowship, superior to creed and race. What is the secret of their power and attraction ?

The answer is clearly to be found in the needs to which they minister. To an age emerging from the materialism of the nineteenth century Christian Science brings the kindling conviction of the supremacy of spirit over matter. To a psychological generation like our own it offers an education in healthy thinking. To a nervous and high-strung folk it

the oblivion to which we have banished
it. It is a poor corrective of a misuse,
which has turned a sacrament of life
into a preparation for death, entirely
to ignore the spiritual ministries of
healing which Christ has left to His
Church. It would be a mighty evangelistic reinforcement could we return to the
simple faith of the first Church, and send
our priests to the sick-bed as St. James
bids us, not only to teach resignation
and to prepare men for death, but to
lay their hands upon the sick that they
might recover, and to bring them in a
sacrament the gift of restoration to
health as well as forgiveness of sins.

Theosophy is equally built upon our
omissions. Had we taught men the
Catholic Faith they would not be at the
mercy of every blast of vain doctrine.
Had we trained them in the inner
ways of meditation and prayer and
opened to them the divine resources
of the sacramental life, we should have
fed the inner hunger of their spirits,

nor would they then have gone empty away.

As for Spiritualism, had prayer for the departed taken its true place amongst us, and our Eucharistic fellowship with the departed in the pleading of that Sacrifice, wherein death is destroyed and the gulf between the living and the dead is bridged, been the common knowledge and the common reliance of every Churchman, and not the privilege of a favoured few, many a one would never have known that heartache which sent them for comfort to the doubtful methods of the spiritualistic *séance*. If we block up the wells of God in our sheltered garden of the Church, we must not complain when we wake up to discover that they are breaking out by the wayside over the hedge.

Nor can we lightly clear our conscience as a Church in the face of the alienation of Labour. Two witnesses, each in his own way, have recently directed our attention towards the Church's attitude to Labour, Cardinal Bourne and the Bishop of Peterborough, in words that deserve our most serious consideration. It is, I am persuaded, only too evident that Labour has little use for the Church ; is, indeed, largely hostile to it, though it has no hostility to Jesus Christ. Both our Archbishops have been brought into personal contact with manifestations of an unfriendly democracy. The Archbishop of York, in a town's meeting at Newcastle, had to hear the reproach of a Labour leader that the Church had done nothing to help the miners of the North to better their condition. At Woolwich —in a scene significant enough in the fair and faithful account of it which appeared in *The Church Times* from the pen of the late Mr. King to need neither embellishment nor exaggeration — the Archbishop of Canterbury witnessed, though he could scarcely have heard, a speaker to the same effect who persisted in lifting up his voice hard by while he himself was preaching in the open.

" It is undeniable," says the Evangelistic Report, " that the Church's own record stands in its way to-day. Labour is conscious that it has worked its way upward with little help from the Church. Old abuses, child-labour, intolerable conditions of housing, and the monstrous evil of the slums, long continued to exist with scarcely a protest from the Church at large, whose silence and inaction have been the more marked by contrast with the single voices raised within its own borders. The deplorable result is that the Church is now regarded by thousands as the hereditary enemy of the ideals of the working classes." . . . " It is not by adopting the phrases and programmes of the socialism of the day that she will win the workers for Christ, but by exhibiting in her own life the Spirit and Gospel of her Master from whom all that is noble in socialism is directly derived. . . . The Church ought to be distinguished from the world by the type of common life into which her members are drawn, a life of simplicity and self-discipline, of practical fellowship and brotherhood . . . this must be her challenge to the present social order." [1]

But a way of repentance will open

[1] Report on the Evangelistic Work of the Church, pp. 3, 37.

to the Church in the reconstruction of national life which must follow the war. A Church, on fire for social righteousness and justice, will alone be able to evangelise England after the war. It is an ungracious task to speak of the failure of the Church, and it is an ambiguous phrase at the best, for the Church is the Body of Christ, indwelt by His Presence, and Christ fails not. Yet failure there is somewhere when the Church finds itself impotent to make disciples for her Lord, and to communicate His Life to those to whom she is sent. It is not the failure of our Lord but of His Body upon earth, not of the Church but of Churchmen, yet of Churchmen in their corporate capacity. Have not we of the Catholic Church in this land to confess that we have imprisoned and restrained the glory of the Christ in a body paralysed, blind, deaf, voiceless, torn, and bleeding from the wounds of its divisions, and powerless, till it be rebaptized with His Spirit, to do His will? Is not the old prophetic lament of God true of the Church to-day : *Who is blind but my servant, or deaf as the messenger that I sent*? But a day of opportunity, the greatest, it may be, is already dawning before the Church of England, and if she go forward to the new day in the spirit, not of self-sufficiency and pride, but of humility, of penitence, in the spirit of a disciple kindled anew with devotion to his Master, she need not fear the future. Only by a penitent and teachable Church can our race be re-evangelised in the years that are to come. Still we hear His command and are assured of His unfailing Presence in our midst. Pray that we may not prove unworthy of the coming day whose dawn already gilds the hills.

VII

THE GOSPEL OF THE PRESENCE

I<small>T</small> is the essence of an evangel that it be news, and good news at that. Its message must break upon the mind fresh and bracing as the dawn of a new day. To be a disciple of the Kingdom of Heaven is to have discovered a perennial fountain of originality, to possess a gospel which, while it is essentially the same, one and continuous in every age, is yet found to hold within itself, as the centuries pass, the satisfaction of the deepest and the newest needs of each succeeding generation. What adventures and surprises the evangelistic movements of Christian history recall ! Peter the Hermit proclaiming the Crusades; Francis with his evangel of poverty;

Suso and Tauler recalling the men of
Rhineland to God with a deep and
tender mysticism; Fox preaching the
Inner Light up and down England;
Wesley by a message of conversion converting men in thousands; the Oxford
Fathers bringing back the Sacraments
to a hungry land; and Moody banishing
men's terrors by a new insistence on the
love of the Father. Yet all these evangels were essentially one; the novelty is
only in the mind of hearer and preacher;
they are concentric, and their centre
is Jesus Christ. Truly the evangel of
Christ has proved through history to be
no stagnant pool. It comes down the
reaches of time like a fresh stream from
the Galilean hills where it rose, now
halting awhile in shadowy pools, but
only to leap forward over the rocks in
impetuous cascades, widening as it goes,
gathering into one great volume the
world's devotion to the Person of Jesus
Christ. If, then, the Church of England
is to bend itself to the task of re-evangel-

ising the English people, of leading our
race into the conscious and loyal discipleship of our Blessed Lord, it is of the
first importance that we should ask ourselves what is the presentation of the one
Lord Christ to which our own generation will most readily respond ; what, in
a word, is the message to the age.

I

There is indeed in the literature of our
time, and in the letters and writings that
are reaching us from the front, a varied
and converging testimony that the conception of God which alone will satisfy
our modern hunger is the thought of
Him which does not need to seek Him
above the stars, but has discovered Him
within ; that the Christ for whom our
age is asking is the Christ present. In
theological language, men are longing
for the realisation of the Divine Immanence. A few years ago immanence was
a word much upon our lips. Dr. Illing-
worth had brought it back to the

remembrance of the learned, and the distinguished preacher who at that time occupied the pulpit of the City Temple, whom now we welcome as one of ourselves, had introduced it to the multitude. The eager acceptance of this doctrine of God and Christ was significant. Crudities were forgiven or undetected, here was a conception of God which appealed directly to the mind of a generation just escaping from the deadening pressure of the narrowly materialistic science of the nineteenth century. When, however, the more critical theologians began to suggest that this doctrine lay dangerously near to Pantheism, many preachers of the Divine Immanence hastily retreated to more secure and familiar ground. But the people are still hungry for that presentation of God which St. Paul offered to the Athenians on Mars Hill—*God in whom we live and move and have our being.*

War-time has strikingly brought to light this hunger for the sense of a God

Who is not only near but within. My
first witness is Mr. Wells. I call him
not as a theologian ; that he is not ; but
he is an accurate observer and a good
barometer of the spiritual consciousness
of the average untheological Englishman
of our time in his eager and bold thought
of God, and in his hunger for immediate
spiritual experience. He is describing
the coming of God to the soul.

" Then suddenly," he writes, " in a little
while, in His own time, God comes. This
cardinal experience is an undoubting immediate sense of God. It is the attainment of an
absolute certainty that one is not alone in oneself. It is as if one were touched at every
point by a Being akin to oneself, sympathetic,
beyond measure wiser, steadfast, pure in aim.
It is completer and more intimate, but it is like
standing side by side with and touching some
one we love very dearly and trust completely.
It is as if this Being bridged a thousand mis-
understandings and brought us into fellowship with a great multitude of other people.
' Closer is He than breathing, and nearer than
hands and feet.' The moment may come
while we are alone in the darkness, under the

stars, or while we walk by ourselves, or in a crowd, in the sinking ship or in tumult of the battle : . . but after it has come our lives are changed. God is with us and there is no more doubt of God. Thereafter one goes about the world like one who was lonely and has found a lover."

What is this but the realisation of the holy immanence of God ? There is no Pantheism here. It is indeed precisely what Pantheism is not ; for it is the vivid and the personal consciousness of a vivid and a personal God.

II

Again, the chaplains in their evidence from the front tell us that religious feeling under fire is not so much the desire of salvation as it is the need of companionship. This is, of course, a verdict of clergymen, but it is singularly borne out by the writer who by common confession has best interpreted the soul of the British citizen soldier, that is, of the average Englishman. With the insight of rare sympathy and penetrating genius Donald Hankey, not a priest, but " The Student in Arms," is describing " how an Englishman prays." He pictures his Englishman lying wounded.

" He lay in the long grass between the lines with an incessant and throbbing pain. A whizz-bang had caught him. All the afternoon he lay still. Would any one find him when it was dark or would he be left to die ? He was cut off from his fellow-men as surely as if he had been on a desert island, and he felt somehow as if he was out of his element, and was launched, a tiny pigmy soul, on the sea of immensity. Eternity and Infinity were so pitiless and uncomprehending, yet, after all, he had the advantage of them. For all his pigmy ineffectiveness, he was of finer stuff than they. At least he could feel. There was that in him which was not in them—God. He whispered softly, ' God everywhere.' Then into his tired brain came a new phrase : ' Underneath are the Everlasting Arms.' "

Here again we discover the Englishman's hunger for the doctrine of the holy immanence of God, no longer a dogma for theologians to wrestle over, but brought out of the conflict of the academy and the schools on to the battlefield of life.

But we do not need to go to the men of letters. In our own treasuries we have the letters of men who are our friends. Here is one written from Egypt, on the edge of the desert.

"One thing sure, God is with me, and really, when on lonely outpost duty, I have some of the best times of my life and I could cry aloud with joy, but not emotion."

Here, again, is a soldier in England, convalescent after a dangerous wound received in France.

"I lay out in No Man's Land for hours," he writes; "I believed I was dying, but I was happy. I knew I was not alone, Jesus Christ was with me. What would I not give here in England for such a sense of His Presence as I had then?"

He has gone out again, and the sense of the Presence returns to him in times of peril.

"A Boche is bombing round us as I write, so we are set in the midst of many and great dangers, but I do feel surrounded by loving prayers in the times of danger, and am conscious of God's Presence in special times of stress."

Such letters leave us in no doubt what the message for our age must be, or how Christ Jesus should be set before the men of England to-day.

But let us not imagine that it is only in France that this hunger for the holy immanence of our Lord gnaws at the heart of men and women. At Woolwich, in the crusade, two pictures were eagerly bought by the women munition workers —" The Great Sacrifice " and " The White Comrade." These two pictures are both interpretations of the holy Presence of the Lord Christ ; in the one a soldier is helping his wounded comrade back to safety ; the Christ Himself, radiant in light, unseen by him, is at his side as he serves his brother's need. In the other the soldier has made the supreme sacrifice, and the figure of the Crucified is seen in the dawning light, so close that

the lad's hand rests upon the feet of
Christ. We are reminded of the prayer
that we have learned to offer for their
souls : " By the sacrifice of their earthly
life may they be brought nigh to the
Sacrifice of Thy well-beloved Son by
Whom the world is redeemed." It is
the invisible Christ there presented
which has drawn thousands to buy these
pictures who scarcely articulately knew
what attracted them. Night after night
at Woolwich, and morning by morning
after the long day-shift and the seeming
longer night-shift, after weary hours of
strain and toil upon their dangerous
tasks, girls at work upon munitions were
found willing to come into the little
chapel of their hostel for half an hour
before they took the rest so sorely needed
for their bodies. What was it that
attracted them ? It was the message
of the invisible presence of Him who
said to the toilers of Galilee, *Come unto
Me and I will give you rest*. The
silence, the living silence, of His holy

presence became a thing that might be felt, and they were discovering there, as His rest flowed round them, the very thing for which their hearts were hungering.

III

The message to the age is Jesus—no other; and no other presentation of Him is sufficient. Jesus, not as a far-away figure of history seen through the pages of the Gospels, not as the final and still far-off Judge throned in glory, but Jesus present here and now, at every hour and in every place, immediately accessible, within; and in this Christ-presence it is strange if we do not discern the presence of the Infinite, of the transcendent God. Who but the Infinite can dwell at the centre of every living soul? Transcendence and Immanence are in no conflict. Either without the other could not be.

This is, indeed, how Jesus Christ Himself bade us think of Him. Here lay the necessity for the forty days of the first Eastertide. The men who for three glorious years had known Him in the intimacy of familiar friendship, under terrestrial limitations and conditions, must pass by gentle degrees from the glowing memories of the old intercourse to the heavenlier and the deeper know-ledge of the same Master, mystically, spiritually present. Six miraculous weeks in which the sense of His invisible presence grew upon their consciousness. Did they walk by a country road, He at any moment might join them. Did they meet in the security of the Upper Room, His Form might recompose itself before their eyes, and the old familiar and remembered promise, *Where two or three are gathered in My Name there am I,* be thus visibly fulfilled. The mists of the morning that hung upon the lake-shore might melt, only to reveal His presence—a presence at once familiar yet amazing, so human that they still might look upon His wounds, yet with

96

increasing clearness of perception recognised as the presence of God.

Immanental teaching has its perils, but they are the consequences of its truth. Language and imagery inevitably fail man when he attempts to express his consciousness of an infinite God in the rough coinage of words, and this inadequacy of all human speech is fruitful of misunderstanding and error, but we may not therefore decline to seek expression for that infinite Reality of which, however imperfectly, we are aware. We must take the risks of speech. The Church of Christ has never feared, as she fulfilled her teaching duty to the world, to tread the very precipice-edge of error. It is indeed her daring that has proved the safeguard of her orthodoxy. What risks of tritheism she took as she slowly and deliberately enunciated her faith in the Triune. But her creeds are the record of her faithful care to be true to whole experience of God into which Christ's revelation of Him had carried

97   H

her. Knowing God as the Fount and
Origin of life, providing for the necessities
of His creatures, compassionate to for-
give, extending His love freely to every
man without partiality of race or religion,
she names Him *Father*; finding Him
incarnate, sharing our human struggle
and pain, she dares to name God *Son*;
aware of His presence, invisible, universal, immediate as the air, the principle
of our life, the light of our knowledge,
the truth, the abiding reality in whom
we live out our life in time and eternity,
she names God *Spirit*. Glorying in the
paradox she affirms that Father, Son,
and Spirit are no shifting aspects of His
Being, no mere appearances which the
infinite assumes to finite sight, but the
eternal realities of an ineffable Personality, undivided yet unsolitary, a Trinity
that is One only God. Nor need we
hesitate to affirm the Divine Immanence
to a generation open to such a gospel of
God in any fear lest the divine Transcendence should escape men, or the sense of

a personal God be lost in Buddhistic
vacuities or pantheistic fogs. The
Christian doctrine of the Immanence is
the strongest bulwark of the personality
of God. He who has found Christ in
his soul is well secured against Nirvana.
His spiritual consciousness is all of personality, of the presence of a divine Personality in Whom he himself lives with a
new fulness of personal life in a relationship of conscious love and devotion. If,
as we are instructed, the capacity for
fellowship is the crown of personality,
truly it is in the relation of Christ immanent that fellowship attains its zenith
by the discovery of His perpetual
presence in the soul, its life, light, and
love.

St. John has set down for us his own
identification of His Master with these
qualities which most of all transcend
all but the Infinite. *I am the Light of
the world ; he that cometh to Me shall
not walk in darkness but shall have the
light of life.* And this light is for St.

John the universal birthright of man. *The light that lighteth every man that cometh into the world. . . . I am come that ye might have life. . . . I am the Bread of Life . . . as I live by the Father, so he that eateth Me shall live by Me.* There is no mistaking the significance of such a presence as this. It is the presence of God, universal, immanent. All infinity of Being is in this Christ-presence which the disciple who once leant upon His breast identifies as the presence of his Master, Jesus. And lest we should think that the Fourth Gospel was herein but the dream of an old man, mingling with his memories the musings and the longings of a lifelong devotion, there stands St. Matthew's setting of the Church's evangelistic charter : *All power is given unto Me in heaven and in earth; go ye, therefore. . . . Lo, I am with you always, even unto the end of the world.*

Those for whom the holy immanence of God is a conception which flows from the discovery of the ever-present Lord Christ are then, as we believe, in no danger of wandering away into oriental mists. Their whole experience is personal and of a Person. Nor is this any new message. It is St. John's, it is St. Paul's, it is Christ's own ; yet new perhaps as an evangelistic appeal and infinitely welcome. What power there is in it !—power to convert, power to redeem. With what dignity and worth life is invested, stained though it be, thus to discover deep within the soul, even of the sinner, the fresh springs of purity and light ! What new hope, what impulse to repentance, what incentive to resolve, lie in the words, *Christ in you, the hope of glory* ! It was so Christ came to sinners, drawing near, bringing them His presence with open arms ; and His coming and His presence converted. He husbanded all His denunciations for the insincere religious, but to sinners how little He spoke of sin ! —and when He did, as in the fifteenth chapter of St. Luke, the stupidity of sin is forgotten in the love of the Shepherd, and its cruelty and ingratitude are lost in the depths of the Father's welcome.

Of what use to go out into the streets of modern England offering pardon before men are conscious of the Presence which awakens the sense of their need of pardon ? In the past, evangelistic movements offered men escape from impending doom. " Rescue the perishing ! " sang the mission choir at the corners of the streets where the poor live ; but now men do not believe in impending doom. They are not afraid of perishing : hell is a forgotten or discredited terror for them. Fear itself is resented by the best of them, almost by all, as an impertinent intrusion into the dignity of a self-possessed life. Today safety is less attractive than sacrifice. Men had best live dangerously in days like these if they would keep their self-respect. But those who are

102

repelled by evangelistic threatenings are attracted by a gospel which brings them to the sense of the Presence ; there they will discern their sin.

It is, unhappily, true that there are many in England whose theology is not better informed than the Persian poet's—

Folk of a surly tapster tell,
And daub his visage with the smoke of hell—
They talk of some strict testing of us—" Pish !
He's a good fellow and 'twill all be well."

A fool's confidence is this ; an idle and a perilous dream. It costs more to redeem a soul. He that has drawn evil into his being and made it his own is not lightly to be delivered in the presence of that Light, which, being the light of an infinite purity and a ruthless love, burns whatsoever defileth till it be consumed. Through what fires of the Spirit must the sin-stained soul pass in the hands of the heavenly Refiner ! But the fire that He kindles, He kindles in His own heart ; as St. Catherine has taught us, it is the fire of His love. It is His

Presence progressively perceived and embraced. There have been those who said that the Divine Immanence could never convince of sin. The very contrary is the truth. Only " His Presence and His very Self can flesh and blood refine." The sense of sin is but the reaction of our consciousness to the sense of God. It is the self-discovery which follows upon the discovery of God.

The doctrine of the Holy Immanence leads direct to this God-consciousness. So in experience it has been found. It was in New Zealand that I learned that lesson. In the new world and the new age if you show men God they will see their sins, and if you cannot, it is beating the air to denounce them. We had been warned before we went out to expect to find in that land little or no consciousness of sin. What we did find was an amazing hunger for God. From that hunger we derived our message. It was not the message that we thought to deliver when we sailed from England ;

nor stressed as we imagined we should stress it ; nor communicated by the old familiar methods to which we missioners had been accustomed. As we went about that land, meeting one another in the train at times, it was surprising to find that experience had led some of us, quite independently of one another, in the same direction. It was an answer to a thousand prayers : God was showing us the message to that new world. It was the message for which the new age everywhere is waiting. It was a Gospel of Christ in man, the Immanence that is the hope of glory.

St. John records an incident in our Saviour's earthly life which interprets for us the converting power of the simple realisation of Christ's Presence. Seeking to embarrass Him by immediate contact with sin, and to test how far He would carry His gospel of unlimited mercy for sinners, that they might have to accuse Him, His enemies one day dragged into the presence of Jesus a woman taken in adultery. "Moses in the law commanded that such should be stoned—what sayest Thou?" Them He rebuked before the inner bar of conscience : "Let him that is without sin amongst you cast the first stone." To the woman He was silent; with a divine courtesy He rebuked her not so much as by a glance. His eyes were cast upon the ground while He wrote in the dust; but His Presence in the silence, the silence which at last none shared but Jesus and the woman, was more converting than rebuke. "Woman," He said to her, using the word by which in supreme moments He addressed our Lady, His dear Mother : "Woman, where are those thine accusers? Hath no man condemned thee?" She said : "No man, Lord." It was a penitent convinced of sin to whom He said : "Neither do I condemn thee; go, sin no more."

VIII

SERVICE AND SACRIFICE

I

HE who discerns the Christ-presence is conscious of a profound moral demand, of the pressure of another will upon his own. The last generation knew that demand as an external ideal more than as an inward pressure, witness John Stuart Mill's advice : " So live that Jesus Christ will approve," or the underlying suggestion of such phrases as : " If Christ came to Chicago." After nineteen centuries it is impossible to name the name of Jesus Christ without challenge to conscience. But to this generation there must be no " if Christ came " ; He is here, He is in me, there-

fore I cannot dishonour His presence.
In the discovery of Christ's presence in
the soul is the interpretation of the
highest of man's endowments which
baffled the evolutionists and biologists
of the last generation. We recognise
in conscience the constraint and pressure
of the will of God reaching us not from
without in an external code or law, but
from within. Conscience, we are bold
to say, is the internal evidence of the
presence of Christ in the soul. Our
Lord Himself expresses the moral challenge of His mystical Presence in two
vivid metaphors drawn from the life of
Palestine in His day—the Yoke and
the Cross. The yoke to an Oriental
conveyed the idea of service, but not of
service in solitude. The root-meaning
of the word yoke, in Greek and in
English, is that which unites two to
a single task. "Take My yoke upon
you" is the call to companionship with
Jesus Christ in the service of humanity.
The message for the age is not only a

certain showing forth of Jesus Christ
but a demand made in His name, and
it will not be the less welcome an
evangel because that demand is high.
We have learnt in England in these
years of war that the call to service has
irresistible attraction. Thousands, nay
millions, have rushed to obey it in a
great wave of enthusiasm for service
which has swept over the land. Men
and women in Army and Navy, in
munition factory, hospital ward, and in
many different ways, have hastened to
get themselves into service and have
found in so doing that life has gained
for them a new dignity, value, and
delight. There is hope for an evangel
which will interpret to our age its new-
found joy in service, and reveal to man
the presence of the Christ which is to be
found in all honest service of humanity.
The forgiveness of sins is not the end of
the evangel. Christ has not finished
with the soul when He has absolved it,
nor has evangelisation done its work

till it has proclaimed Christ as a King calling men to the service of their fellows, which He declares to be service done to Himself: *Inasmuch as ye have done it unto one of the least of these My brethren, ye have done it unto Me.* Here lies the immediate evangelistic duty of the Church; and here the Church has a real contribution to make. She must offer men, in the name of Christ, union with God through service. Her Master was indeed the foremost of all the servants of mankind—"I am among you," He said, "as He that serveth." On every plane of service Christ laboured to supply man's necessity. None ever served his spiritual and intellectual need as did the Christ, and yet He was not content to minister only to mind and soul, nor only to bodily health. He was ready for the menial duties of a slave, and for the tasks of the manual labourer. He did not disdain to call upon the resources of His divine nature to give hungry men a meal. In

110

the upper chamber, in a dramatised
lesson, He taught the Twelve that the
best of all preparations for communion
with Deity was the service of their
fellows, though it be the humblest and
the simplest : *Ye ought also to wash
one another's feet.* Never is the presence of Christ more securely pledged
than when we make His task our own
and are thereby bound to Him in the
fellowship of His yoke. But it is not
only the mystical presence which the
Church must show men in the call to
service, it is the end He had in view.
Christ was possessed by a vision which
dominated His consciousness, was the
theme of His teaching, and the purpose
of His life. It was the vision of the
Kingdom of Heaven upon earth. The
Kingdom of Heaven has often been
thought of as a dream of the life beyond.
In reality as Christ conceived it, it was
heaven realised on earth. Society on
earth directed by the laws of God,
humanity organised for brotherhood and

111

love, justice, truth, righteousness, and peace—what a gospel for a democratic age! It is the dream of the Kingdom of God, seen afar off, that has inspired all that is noble in socialism and may yet end war, realised in part in the League of Free Nations. It is our evangelistic duty to show Christ to the world as the inspiration and the motive power of all service in the cause of humanity, the cause, that is to say, of the Kingdom of Heaven. But the Church must itself, like its Master, be the first servant of man. Not till every altar is recognised as the place of consecration to such service, service understood to be not the less spiritual because its sphere is on the earth, will the Church be the evangelist of this generation. New fields of service will open to the Church after the war. Peace will set free multitudes of young men and young women who, having discovered the dignity and the satisfaction of service, will decline to return to ornamental unemployment. This will

112

be the Church's opportunity. If it can
offer to them work at once human and
spiritual, be it in the rebuilding of
English life in country and town, or the
making of new nations in far-off places
of the Empire, or the education of
African child races, or the emancipation
of the womanhood of India, highest,
most adventurous of all, world evangelisation, the Church will count her volun-
teers in thousands if she sets high enough
the call to service. The discovery of
the Christ-presence in man sets a value
upon every human life, and spiritualises
every form of service. It inspires the
grand ambition, England and the world
for Christ. And many a man will find as
he enlists in the service of Jesus the King
that he cannot serve worthily till he has
found Jesus the Saviour. It is true to
the experience of life that the call to
high and holy tasks is more humbling
than the recollection of our past failures.
The sense of sin is often created by the
attempt to serve ; high vocation has a

way of melting hearts which denunciations do but harden.

II

Our Lord's other symbol is the Cross. *He that taketh not his cross and followeth after Me is not worthy of Me.* It is His invariable condition of discipleship. There was no mistaking its drastic meaning. The cross was an everyday sight in Palestine under the Romans. It was no gilded metaphor of minor self-denials. To us the Cross is more associated with honour than shame. Then it was the ruthless symbol of death in its most cruel, appalling, and disgraceful form. It had the naked reality that war has brought back to the word " sacrifice "—a terrible, inexorable demand. " Christianity is heroism," said La Maréchale.[1] Heroism it is, often, like the heroism of modern war where khaki and mud have replaced scarlet

---

[1] *La Maréchale*, by James Strachan, p. 43. An account of the work of Catherine Booth the younger, who planted the Salvation Army in the slums of Paris at twenty-two.

and gold ; adventure without romance, darkness and horror lit up only by courage and comradeship, by sacrifice and fellowship, by the flash of unconquerable spirit. The religion which will demand the spirit of sacrifice in the name of Christ need have no fears of the future ; it makes an irresistible appeal to this generation when it presents Christ Jesus as He presented Himself to those who desired to be His disciples.

" Gentle Jesus, meek and mild " ; so we learnt to think of Him at our mother's knee, so we have found Him often in the dust of our confessions, so brokenhearted men and women in every age have found a refuge in the Sacred Heart. But is this all ? It is a wonderful gospel of Jesus for stricken souls, but there is more in Christ than this. There is a passage in *John Inglesant* in which the Greek conception of God is contrasted with the Christian :

" They were standing in the Belvedere Gardens in Rome before the statue of Apollo.

Inglesant took from beneath his vest a Crucifix in ivory and held it beside the statue of the god. The one the noblest product of buoyant life, the proudest perfection of harmonious form, the other one worn and emaciated, helpless, dying apparently without power, forgotten by the world. ' Has the Galilean triumphed ? ' asked Inglesant's companion. ' Do you prefer the Christ ? ' "

Ten years ago I tried to answer that question, and to set down wherein lies the victorious appeal of the Crucifix :

" There is no doubt about the answer which comes back from the chamber of sickness or death. It is only in Jesus and in the cross of Jesus that the infinite pity of God is articulate. There is no grief in the whole gamut of sorrow but has its echo in the passion of Christ. No physical torture could exceed the sufferings of the scourging or the crucifying, no spiritual desolation or doubt could be so bitter as that night of the soul which wrung from Jesus the cry, ' Why didst Thou forsake Me ? ' He has explored the depths of mental and physical anguish and His experience is the experience of God. By it we are drawn to God as by nothing else." [1]

[1] *The Self-Revelation of Jesus*, p. 91.

This much I could see ten years ago, and I do not go back upon it. But now I see how diminished a reading of the crucifix is that which sees there only the articulate pity of God. *Sic deus dilexit mundum ;* this has been its meaning to thousands in the years that are gone. This is its everlasting message, but it is not all. Thrice Pilate wrote "King" above the Cross, and now, though never did the world have greater need of the infinite pity than to-day, it discerns in the form of the patient sufferer, the invisible King. It sees on the cross the Hero who by divine right commands. I find myself to-day asking for the crucifix in which, in symbolism more true than any realism, Christ is presented reigning from the tree. The crucifix, which interprets the might and majesty of His courage, the mystic Byzantine crucifix of the King-Priest, robed, crowned, and reigning, the crucifix of the Vexilla Regis : *regnavit a ligno deus*—God reigning from the tree. This

is the crucifix for the youth in the fresh
morning of his manhood, the crucifix
which will show to him the power of the
name of Jesus ; the name which from
the dawn of history was the name of a
conquering hero, the leader, the cap-
tain, of God's people. Here the lad
may see his Lord claiming his manhood
with a royal claim, and like a King
communicating to His subject, whom He
calls to share His royalty of sacrifice,
His own kingly strength. The crucifix
is coming back to England ; old prejudice is dead. Nor are we likely to
fashion our crucifixes after the later
models which emphasise with repellent
realism the physical torture upon which
the gospels refuse to dwell. We are
more in danger of representations of the
crucifix which err upon the side of
weakness. Might we not well return to
the grand original, mystical and regal,
which for centuries was the only known
form of the crucifix ? Or if that may
not be, upon the outer wall of Romsey

118

Abbey there is a tenth-century crucifix, the pride of the Winchester diocese; weather-beaten and rough-handled, the majesty of the Crucified may yet be seen there; the massive brow, the feet set firm, the arms which seem less to sustain the body's weight than to be stretched wide in power and benediction. It is a visible symbol of power in sacrifice, and it is sacrifice which gives power to life and reality to religion, which is indeed the essential act of faith. If faith be testing the reality of the unseen, sacrifice is its supreme expression. From the moment when a man makes his first real sacrifice for an invisible God, his feet touch the rock. Here is the spring of the gaiety and laughter, of the *camaraderie* and brotherhood, of the endurance under drudgery, hardship, wounds, and perils, which our age has witnessed in its soldiers, inarticulate, half-unconscious, it may be, yet sufficient. By sacrifice these men have laid hold upon reality. Biologists inform us that in

119

the last analysis life is self-giving, and death is but the loss of the power of self-abandonment to surrounding life. Our Lord did not deal with biology, but with eternal life, yet He has taught us that this is not less true in eternity. We have witnessed the amazing attraction of sacrifice for our generation. From town and village, office and school, from the houses of the great, from the cottages of the poor, from factory, shipyard, mine, and field, a multitude numbered in millions, women and men, with youth upon their brow in the first vigour of their physical beauty and strength, have answered to the call of sacrifice. They thought that the voice that called them was England, but when England called for truth, for justice, and freedom, for the strong to deliver the weak, to bring life and liberty to the oppressed, she called in the name of Christ.

IX

THE SACRAMENTAL TIDE

THE soldier has left us in no doubt that the message to this age must be a sacramental message. One of the spiritual discoveries of the war has been the appeal which Holy Communion makes to men at the Front, who at home scarcely knew of its existence. Here is the testimony of the unknown writer who contributes to the columns of the *Times* on Saturdays articles which many look for with expectation :

" When the soldier seeks for courage and hope in his faith, nothing makes so moving an appeal to him as Holy Communion. Nor is the appeal found only in one manner of keeping the feast. The Russian peasant and the French Catholic, the Anglican and the Free Churchman, though they inherit varied ways of re-

membering the Lord's death, alike find in the
Holy Communion a new and solemn appeal."

With this testimony agree two Presbyterian chaplains :

" The opinions of chaplains contradict each
other on many points, but there is an impressive agreement that the great Sacrament has
come to mean more to the men, and that
Presbyterian and Nonconformist communions
must alter their practice in relation to it.   It
has come to be seen afresh as the supremest of
all occasions in the ordinary life of the Church,
in which a man may draw nigh to God and be
satisfied of the real presence of his Saviour."

Nor is it only among chaplains at the
front.   Here is Dr. Forsyth speaking to
an evangelical conference at Mansfield
College :

" We should not forget that the greatest
example of Church unity, the Roman Church,
has a standing miracle at the centre of its
worship.   The Mass is not a mere rite, but a
creative miracle."

Or there is Dr. Orchard at the King's
Weigh House finding a remarkable response as he celebrates with ceremonial

enrichments Saints - day and Sunday Eucharists. The younger generation of Nonconformists, we are told, is hungry for the Sacrament. Everywhere one may see signs of return to sacramental worship.

" The Eucharist," says Mr. Milner White, in *The Church in the Furnace*, " has proved itself to thousands to whom it was scarcely a name before. At officers' conferences where the officers are plain men who do not themselves communicate often and prefer the Matins tradition of Sunday observance, there is astonishing consent that the Eucharist henceforth must be the chief service of the day and put in the chief place of time and honour. Be it repeated, it is the sturdy, uncontroversial, unceremonial, central body of Church people who speak thus."

There are still plenty of able defenders of Sunday Matins ready to demand the old Hanoverian non-sacramental type of Anglicanism, but the tide is against them. The younger generation would seem to be returning to what after all may claim to be the Christian ideal of worship since it is unquestionably Christ's ordinance. What is it that attracts ?   Let a chaplain answer :

"It is reality and not High Church bias that makes men prefer the Lord's Supper to a service invented three hundred years ago ; the meal of the brotherhood of Jesus is more to them than a choir office."

Is it strange that a generation which seeks the Christ-presence should find its satisfaction in that rite which, however bare its setting, is first and last the Sacrament of the presence of Christ ? Is it strange that men who have felt the irresistible attraction of the call to sacrifice should find in a service, which is the adoration of sacrifice in God and the perpetual pleading of the supreme sacrifice of Jesus, that which answers to their deepest need ?   " The memory of a divine sacrifice, the communion with a living Lord, it is the story with a death in it and in some mysterious way the soldier feels that Death spreads its healing over him," says the anonymous

writer in the *Times*. And if plain men
reach no further than that, the simplest
can perceive the grandeur of a faith
which finds in a solemn act of human
fellowship some strange and wonderful
gift of divine life. To a generation
awaking to discover the spiritual through
the visible, and, above all, open to the
idea of fellowship, this brotherhood,
expressed not in words but in the solemn
action of the Sacrament, would seem to
make an inevitable appeal. It is an
appeal that is at once new and old.
New, for to the great majority of Churchmen it has almost been unknown, and
certainly strange and unfamiliar, yet
old, for it offers the attraction of im-
memorial antiquity and the reassurance
of the spiritual experience of the vast
and overwhelming majority of Christian
men through nineteen centuries.

But as we take heart, we to whom
by God's mercy the sacramental mysteries have these long years been the
very stay of our life in Christ, are there

no lessons for us ? How shall we go out to gather in all, as many as we shall find, to the marriage feast of the King's Son ? What welcome shall we offer them ? How shall we open the way ? How remove whatever of misunderstanding or prejudice yet hinders ? I find that this new sacramental feeling is eager to disown any magical or exclusive sacramental appeal. The safeguard against the magical conception of the Sacrament lies in the emphasis that we must always lay upon the moral disposition of him who approaches the altar : the wedding-garment of penitence and pardon. As a safeguard against a narrowly exclusive conception of the sacraments, do we not need to bring forward that most ancient and weighty Catholic principle, *Deus non obligatur sacramentis suis*—God is not tied down to His own sacraments—to bring it from the background, out of brackets, so to speak, to its rightful place as a vital interpretation of sacramental grace ?

126

Here we disown in a single sentence a ground of misunderstanding that has stood in the way of thousands. Catholicism, be it ever remembered, is always more concerned to affirm than to deny; it is the genius of Catholicism to affirm, as of Protestantism to deny. It affirms that the baptized is the child of God, it does not thereby deny that God is the Father of the unbaptized; it assures the penitent of his absolution, it does not deny that the unabsolved penitent is forgiven; it adores the Christ in the Sacrament, but it does not deny His Presence beyond the Sacrament; it affirms that here is the Bread of Life, but it does not deny that man may feed upon Christ in other ways. True Catholicism sees in the Sacrament the extension of the Incarnation. Once in time and place God was incarnate, but St. John does not so conceive of the Word made Flesh as to suggest that only in the thirty-three years of the incarnate life was God in man or in

127

the world. In that life, the presence of God Who dwells in every man, was focussed at a point in time. It is so with the Sacrament. In the altar mystery is focussed, recognised, and adored the universal presence of the Son of God, and I shall not the less discern His presence elsewhere because I have knelt to adore the Christ in the Sacrament. As the Angelus rings in the valley below, the majesty of the unseen Presence of which the glittering snows upon the heights are sign and sacrament, is focussed and intensified for me by yonder distant bell. Here is salt and safeguard to keep our Catholicism broad, sane, and evangelistic. Sacerdotalism is only false when it claims to be indispensable to communion with God, and the sacramental Presence is only exaggerated when men argue from it a virtual absence of the Lord Christ where the Sacrament is not. Here is the open road to a sacramental faith. To him for whom " earth's crammed with God and every common bush aflame," it is but the crown and glory of the material world that, at the touch of the Spirit and at the word of Christ, the divine Presence should in the Bread and Wine of the altar be focussed with an intensity of power corresponding to the loftiness of the divine purpose.

And, with breadth, war is restoring the sense of proportion. In particular I might instance the effect of war conditions upon the age-old and venerable custom of fasting Communion. It would appear that at the Front, and even in the home-camps, fasting Communion is in abeyance for the duration of the war. It is to be remarked here that our chaplains find themselves following the lead of their Roman Catholic brethren. Technically, each Communion is, I suppose, regarded as the *viaticum* which so often, at the Front, it may actually become, for which no fast was ever required. But in reality it is the recognition that the receiving of the Sacrament

is more vital than the most ancient of
traditional customs. It is the command
of God, " Take, eat," prevailing over any
tradition that might seem under war
conditions to make it of none effect ; it
is rigidity become elastic under pressure,
particularly under the necessity of the
soldier's Communion. Will the chaplains who have passed through this
experience ever again feel as in pre-war
days on this matter ? Certain it is that
their present action is hailed with universal approval.

" Frankly and gladly," says Mr. Milner
White, who writes as a Catholic, " accepting
the situation, many of us have come now to
afternoon, evening, and night Communion.
Such occasions draw throngs of men sobered
and earnest. We have guarded the occasion
by declaring it a war emergency not to be
looked for at home, and by instructing care-
fully through the service, but it is without
doubt due to this evening Communion, or to
the instruction given to them, that the Blessed
Sacrament has grown larger in the love of
warriors." [1]

---

[1] *The Church in the Furnace*, p. 208.

Few would deny the value of a rule which associates self-sacrifice with Communion, and acts as a constant check upon spiritual sloth and bodily laziness. There are few who would not feel that an innate and natural reverence is here accordant with traditional custom, but on the other hand are there not peace conditions in industrial and agricultural England, for women as well as for men, in which rigorous insistence on the absolute fast from the previous midnight constitutes a practical barrier to any but the most infrequent and rare receiving of the Sacrament? Are we in the face of war experience to meet the multitudes, who are already drawn towards the Sacrament and attracted by its appeal, with rigorist restrictions, which must seem to them, even if they do not to ourselves, to set human tradition above divine command? And the experience of war-time necessities may perhaps throw light upon our past manner of presenting the sacramental

131

mysteries to our fellow - countrymen
which may save us from mistakes in our
present endeavour to use to the full the
evangelistic opportunity that now is
offered to us. It must be admitted that
while in many ways the influence of the
Oxford Movement has been predominant
in the more recent history of the Church
of England, in one respect, and that
vital, it has failed It has not succeeded,
save in a small minority of our Churches,
in placing the Holy Sacrament at the
very centre of our Anglican worship as
the recognised spiritual obligation of the
Lord's Day. It is at least possible that
the over-insistence upon the fast before
Communion accounts in part for this disappointing result. The rule, which had
become obsolete, was revived and en-
throned in a dominant place as if it were
the very essence of Catholic life. As a
method of sacramental propaganda this
procedure would appear to have been im-
prudent. Once men had learnt to discern
the Presence, natural reverence would

have commended to their conscience so instinctive and devout an observance, though in truer proportion, and subordinate to the main purpose of the Sacrament. But until men have found Christ in the mystery, the arbitrary insistence upon the traditional rule is likely to repel rather than to attract them to the altar, and what they will feel to be disproportionate emphasis upon it may have the unfortunate result of surrounding the Blessed Sacrament with materialistic and mechanical suggestion. Desirable as it is to restore discipline to our Christian life, it is less clear that this is the wisest point at which to begin this restoration. We may well beware of thus discouraging the present wide-spreading movement of mind in a sacramental direction.

Let me repeat that it is in the cause of evangelisation, and as an act of charity to the multitudes upon whom Christ has compassion, that I should be prepared to consent to such a departure. However rudimentary and ill-instructed their hunger for the heavenly Bread, we may not send away fasting those who come from far lest they faint by the way.[1] Such an innovation as evening Communion, under whatever conditions, ought to be no private enterprise. The machinery of dispensation is, it is true, obsolete, but short of provincial action, I should regard episcopal regulation as an essential safeguard for a variation from the established practice of Christian history which nothing but necessity could justify. I am in entire agreement with Mr. Neville Talbot's statement in the Report on the Worship of the Church :

" If, as is probable, such enquiry points to the need of Holy Communion in the evening, it will be important to secure that it is always a service by itself, for those who cannot come at other times, and not a sequel to another service from which individuals stay on, on the spur of the moment."

[1] See Appendix, " Dr. Pusey on Fasting Communion."

"His Majesty," said St. Teresa,
"loves courageous souls." Catholicism
need never fear adventure. After all,
there is nothing old that was not once
new, save God alone. Would not our Lord
have said, "The Sacraments are made
for man, not man for the Sacraments"?
So that we keep the mind of Christ, and
act not as seems good in our own eyes
but as we are led by His Spirit to believe
that He would have us act, and I should
like to be able to add as we are guided
by wise and courageous authority, we
shall not fail to show Him to the millions
whose souls are hungry for the Bread
He has left them, who are weary for His
Presence to share their service and carry
them through sacrifice to their crown.
Certain it is we shall never re-evangelise
England unless we can offer men full,
free, and unfettered all that Christ has
left them in the Blessed Sacrament.
But let no man lose heart as he looks
wide over the broad fields of *Ecclesia
Anglicana*, though he find there another

135

way of worship than Christ's own still in possession. The sacramental tide is flowing free.

> Far hence by many a creek and inlet making
> Comes silent flooding in the main.

X

THE ROOTED SORROW

Canst thou not minister to the mind diseased ;
Pluck from the memory a rooted sorrow,
Raze out the written troubles of the brain ;
And, with some sweet oblivious antidote ;
Cleanse the stuffed bosom of that perilous stuff,
Which weighs upon the heart ?

Macbeth.

IF the Church is to welcome the multitudes back to the Sacrament, she must know how to remove the inner barriers in mind and conscience which keep men from the altar. Vague and inarticulate as are the sacramental ideas of the average Englishman, they include certain simple yet deeply-rooted convictions which cannot be ignored since they rest upon a recognition of the sanctity of the Sacrament. He feels that to receive

137

Holy Communion would require of him a higher standard of conduct. He himself judges other men who communicate by such a standard, and were he a communicant he would expect others so to judge him. Bad language, for example, gambling, and a certain free and easy relationship to womenfolk short of definite immorality would, he perceives, assume a very different character were he a communicant, though otherwise they lie light upon his conscience.

Further, he shrinks from setting up to be religious, and detests hypocrisy beyond everything, so, though he can see that Communion is a good thing, to which ultimately he might wish to attain, he hangs back, in the fear that he cannot, in the rough and tumble of everyday conditions, live up to its demand. In our desire to meet his need we must guard against injuring or offending the dim reverence for holy things and the deep regard for truth which is the foundation of an Englishman's religion.

138

But it ought not to be impossible to set before him another view of Holy Communion than this, which is at bottom so self-regarding. Only a Pharisee could imagine himself fit for Communion if his own goodness were the qualification. Our Lord's answer to those who criticised His free consorting with the sinful and irreligious is not irrelevant. "*They that be whole have no need of a physician, but they that are sick. . . . I came not to call the righteous but sinners to repentance.*" It is as men draw nearer to Him that they begin to feel the attraction of a higher ideal of life, and to draw from Him the moral and spiritual strength to attain it. And, moreover, we may here recall Father Tyrrell's warning in *Oil and Wine*, that, in our insistence upon the deeper and more mysterious aspects of the Sacraments, the simpler are in danger of being forgotten. The Eastern symbolism of breaking bread with another, as a pledge of fidelity and comradeship, or the simple calling to

mind of His " love which was carried to
the extremity of death—to the rending
of the body and the pouring out of
the blood," these are elementary ideas
within the reach of all, yet they are of
the essence of the Sacrament, and they
might prove to be a bridge from the
false reverence, which declines the Sacrament through the sense of self-distrust,
to a real though still imperfect recognition of its necessity to Christian discipleship. They would at least help men to
think of the Sacrament from the standpoint not of self but of Christ.

This alone would not touch the hindrance most deeply rooted in the conscience. When a man's better self is
awakened, and, it may be, in danger or
extremity he becomes conscious of his
need of God, and the Holy Sacrament
begins to make a new and powerful
appeal to him, if in his memory there are
old sins, secret but unforgotten, or more
recent falls which stand between him and
the Sacrament, his chief evangelistic

140

need is confession. He shrinks from Communion as he is ; he knows little of the ways of prayer and penitence, and of direct communion with the source of forgiveness and peace. An evangelistic Church is failing in its duty to him if that gift of her Lord which directly answers to his need is hidden or withheld. A human ear sealed by inviolable secrecy, a wise and understanding sympathy, a word of power carrying to his heart with the authority of Christ the assurance of his pardon, open to him the realisation of divine forgiveness, and the certainty of his restoration to the Christian fellowship. The chaplains are explicit in their demand.

"I am more than ever convinced," writes one, "of the absolute necessity in the Church of some sort of private confession."

A naval officer writes to the same effect :

"I am not what is called a ritualist, I was brought up an evangelical, but I feel certain

that we need to teach confession more boldly
to our men and boys."

There is no fear that England will
ever submit to the spiritual tyranny
of compulsory confession. That bogey
may be relegated to limbo. But the
time has come when plain men see that
confession is good for the soul, and that
it is the business of the Church to make
the best and wisest provision for the
satisfaction of this genuine human necessity. The demand for the liberty of
voluntary confession is not to be denied.
Every doctor hears confessions, not to
mention schoolmasters, lawyers, and all
men worth their salt whose business
deals with life. But not every man who
is the recipient of confidences which
reveal failure, error, and sin, can bring
the same relief and strength to the
burdened mind. Like Lady Macbeth's
physician, they know that there is a
region of distress which lies beyond
their reach. But the priest hears these
secrets not merely as friend and coun-

sellor, but as the representative of the
fellowship of the Church, as the ear of
the Body of Christ, and he knows himself
to be empowered to speak in the name
of Christ's Body and therefore of Christ.
He speaks with a note of assurance and
authority, when he absolves, which psychologically and spiritually is of in-
calculable value and power in effecting
that inner transformation of consciousness by which the soul is remade.
No evangelisation which ignores this
divinely-given ministry can hope to be
adequate to the spiritual needs of the
age.

With the wider use of the liberty of
sacramental confession there comes from
the laity an increasing demand for its
better regulation by authority. Men
who are to exercise so sacred and intimate a ministry need a fuller preparation
than common-sense and good intentions
afford. The newly-ordained priest may
be reluctant, without more experience of
life and of priestly ministry in general,

143

to embark on this difficult, delicate, and
responsible duty, but it is doubtful
whether, as things stand, he could posi-
tively refuse a request to receive a
confession. Lay-folk may reasonably
ask for assistance from the authorities
of the Church in the choice for themselves
and their families of spiritual guides.
Though there is knowledge of human
nature in the Prayer-Book suggestion
that men should be free to choose the
" discreet and learned minister " to
whom " they may open their grief," yet
it ought to be possible for the Church
to provide that in every district some
such minister was readily accessible,
specially accredited for this duty. " Discreet and learned " implies both training
and personal fitness. We look to the
theological colleges in the future to
provide more adequate training for this
essential ministry than in the past, and
to our Fathers in God to do the rest.

XI

THE GOSPEL IN THE OPEN

THE latest biography of Francis Xavier relates how in the early days in Italy he would run through the streets waving his hat in the air, crying, " Come and hear the word of God." The first seat served him as a pulpit, or he would get the loan of a bench and put it in the middle of the square and preach to the town. Great was the number of people who gathered to the sermon, we read, on account of its novelty, and great was the fruit. Evangelisation has a natural affinity with the open air. Our Lord Himself preached out of doors. Certainly in England to-day, where declining church-going is accompanied by a readiness to hear about God and Christ, if the

news of Him be carried into the open,
and particularly if it be given by a
layman or a laywoman, it is undoubtedly
a necessity of the time. But open-air
evangelisation is not to be limited to
preaching in the open. We need to
carry out of doors something of the
converting atmosphere of the Unseen
Presence which Christian worship can
convey. *Fête Dieu* has lessons for us,
although, under the prevailing conditions
of religious belief in England, charity and
reverence preclude the desire to employ
its method, the procession of the Blessed
Sacrament. Yet few who have ever
spent Corpus Christi abroad but must
have realised its impressive power in a
country where the faith of the people
is predominantly sacramental. One
such day I recall in Echternach in the
grand duchy of Luxemburg—unhappy
Luxemburg, first to be trampled beneath
the iron heel of Germany! The houses
spontaneously decorated, the altars at
the corners of the streets and in the

146

market-place, the great procession in which all ages and all classes joined, from the children in their toy vestments to grey-bearded grandfathers, wandering for two hours under the blazing June sunshine, singing their hymns of praise and adoration in the intervals of repeated litanies and rosaries, and bearing the symbol of the Presence past the houses of the people, through the familiar streets into the market-place. Its effect was to bring the highest of mysteries into immediate contact with the daily life of the people. It seemed as though that day Christ was the Guest of every home in Echternach ; for a day religion dominated life and spread over it the thrill of wonder and joy. At noon, when the procession, weary and hot, returned for the final Te Deum to the crowded cathedral, which indeed could not contain them, the climax of their adoration found noble expression as the old Latin rolled down the aisles to its stern Ambrosian chant : *Pleni sunt coeli*

et terrae majestatis gloriae tuae. There
were tears of devotion on the cheeks of
the rough old peasant at my side and
the light of faith upon his face. If I ask
what was its power, I must answer that
it carried into the streets the living
atmosphere of the spiritual world. To
those simple folk it was Christ Himself,
and which of us would deny their faith,
who passed through their streets and
by their doors, to rest awhile in the
market-place ? Many were the banners
and tokens, but the simple witness of
the hundreds, ready to be seen not
merely walking in procession but at
prayer in the open, was more moving
than all its setting of beauty. Consideration for the religious feeling of the
country forbids such use of the Sacrament in England, and it is a hazardous
act, of doubtful reverence to our Lord's
expressed intention, to use the Sacrament for a purpose so remote from its
institution.

I draw nevertheless three lessons

capable of application to the open-air
work of the Church of England. First,
our open-air witness must be the evidence of the Church's strength and not
its weakness—whole congregations going
out to witness to God in the open. I
cannot bring myself altogether to blame
the English reticence which shrinks from
an over-free speech of God and holy
things, in its hatred of cant and unreality,
but it is time we called upon our people
to the sacred duty of open witness to
their discipleship, to their faith in Christ,
and such an opportunity processions of
witness would afford. Secondly, our processions must carry with them the sense
of God's Presence. That Presence does
not depend upon the Sacrament but
upon the realisation, by those who take
part in them, of Him who is Invisible.
It is vital that that consciousness of
God should, like a cloud of light, over-
shadow the Church's witness in the open.
Thirdly, that processions must be prepared with detail and a thoughtful

organisation. It is no merit, it is only sloth and folly, to neglect the reverent care for the order, beauty, and impressiveness of such acts of corporate witness and prayer. The reproach that the Church of England does not understand these things must be made to cease. If we can carry our people out *en masse* they themselves will catch something of the evangelistic spirit, and will no longer for very shame's sake be content to leave to choir and clergy and a handful of faithful women the duty of evangelisation in the open. It may well be that the chief value of such corporate witness will be its effect upon those who take part in it. It could hardly fail to visualise and so to stimulate the sense of personal responsibility resting upon every member of the Church to bear his part in the evangelisation of his country. There are many signs that it is less by preaching campaigns than by a new realisation of the evangelistic obligations of Christian discipleship among the rank

and file of Churchmen, that England will
be re-evangelised. There is needed a
new spirit in the Church and in the
individual, a new recognition that the
disciple no less than the Church exists
to evangelise. It is startling to recall
how small a place the evangelisation of
our country has occupied hitherto in the
mind of the Church or the individual.
Unnamed in the pulpit, ignored in con-
gresses and conferences, forgotten in our
intercession, it is small wonder that the
average churchman is all but utterly
without the sense that it is his duty, no
less than the priest's, to make disciples
to his Lord and enlist recruits for His
kingdom.

XII

THE EVANGEL OF YOUTH

THE most important element in the
evangelistic field must always be the
young. The Evangelistic Report, it is
true, says nothing about the evangelisation of the young, but that silence is
deliberate and is the recognition of its
supreme importance, since this Committee of Inquiry asks for another, chosen
ad hoc, which will bring expert knowledge
to its consideration. To evangelise the
child is to make him a disciple ; to
educate him in the knowledge of Jesus
Christ, to win for Him the devotion and
the love of His child, and to attach that
child in fealty to the service of His
fellowship, to the Church of which by
baptism he is already a member. It is
152

vitally important that our spiritual education should begin in early life. Childhood is rich in those very qualities to which the gospel of Jesus must always make its appeal. Imagination, faith, self-forgetfulness, generosity, and love are in childhood in their first fresh bloom. In youth the mind is open. It has not hardened into the invincible ignorance of self-sufficiency ; it has no old prejudices ; it is not fast in the rut of convention. The eyes of youth are trained forward ; it is not till middle age that a man begins to whisper to himself : "Here I be, and here I bide." When that lamentable stage is reached, exit the evangelist, for an evangelist, like his Master, must remain dependent upon his hearers' capacity for change. "Change your whole mental outlook and believe the good tidings of God," said Jesus Christ. To repent is to think differently. It is evident that before we can evangelise the child we must understand him, nor shall we understand

153

him unless we are prepared for some moderate study of the psychology of the child-mind. The child always thinks in the concrete, as indeed do all but mature and educated minds. His religion must therefore be presented to him in such wise that he can visualise it. The child, like our Lord Himself, delights in stories. Dramatise and he is interested and influenced ; moralise and he is bored and repelled. Our presentation of religion to the child must therefore be dramatic, visible, and imaginative. Child evangelisation was hard hit by Puritanism, stern school of character though it was. When worship became dull, when the pictures vanished from the walls and windows of the Churches and the saints from their niches, when the Christmas crib, and the Lenten ashes, the palm processions and the Easter pageantry, when beauty in colour, form, and sound ceased from the gatherings of God's people, when middle-age, self-centred and selfishly forgetful of the child, imposed its own dry dulness upon divine worship, and every association of religion became stern, gloomy, ugly, prosaic, frowning and frightening in a well-meant, but mistaken, quest for spirituality, the children were robbed of their spiritual birthright. It is painful to remember through what distorting mirrors children have been compelled to look upon the face of Jesus Christ, for a child's conception of religion must be largely derived from his impressions of public worship. Nor have we who admit old Puritan mistakes always been beyond reproach. It is possible that one of the principal causes of the decline in church-going may be found in the effect of attendance in early life at services wearisome to the child and utterly unsuited to his spiritual needs. Can we venture to maintain that Choral Matins, to which the majority of English children are conducted of a Sunday, is calculated to convey to the child-mind the joy and

155

splendour of religion and the majesty and beauty of God ? To take but a single instance : What is likely to be the effect upon the mind of an intelligent child of the lesson, read *without comment*, of Jacob's lie to his old father on his death-bed, rewarded by the richest bless-ing ? It may be said that a child does not think out questions like these, but that is very far from certain.[1] Children ask questions, and if a child cannot be expected to use his intelligence, it is undesirable to bring him to services the virtue and benefit of which depend upon sustained and vigorous thinking. Not that public worship ought to be brought down to the intellectual level of the child, but there should be nothing to affront his developing moral sense, and if there is still much that escapes his intellectual grasp, at least he should find

[1] Since the recommendation of the Committee of Inquiry into the Worship of the Church in favour of brief explanation before the reading of lessons which require it, this particular stumbling-block will, we may hope, soon be out of the path of our children.

in the service some positive appeal, imaginative and dramatic, yet conveying to him the sense of religious mystery and awe. It is characteristic of the paradox of Christianity that its deepest and highest approach to God is its simplest. The Eucharist is an action ; it is a drama ; it moves to a climax ; it has the sense of a coming, of a Presence, of an offering, it shows forth till He come Christ's great adventure of redemption, not in words but in a simple yet amazing act.

It is not therefore strange that the Eucharist is found in experience to exercise a singular attraction for the young. It is disappointing that at this hour of the day Matins should be so often the morning service of our private and public schools. Some, at least, of those who are responsible for the religion of our public schools themselves regard it as an obsolete ideal of a young man's worship, and many a parent will be found ready to support head-masters

who will initiate reform. There is much
that can be said for Sunday Matins.
It has treasures for the trained mind and
the meditative soul. It has real uses as
a non-committal, non-aggressive, non-
challenging service, adapted to the needs
of many assemblies of loosely-attached
Christians, but he is a bold man who
would assert that it is evangelistic, and
a bolder who would maintain that it is
adapted to the spiritual needs of the
young. Sunday in a Christian school
ought to mean the Lord's service at a
reasonably early hour, with the whole
school present, numbers communicating,
and no restriction forbidding the presence of those who do not yet desire
weekly Communion; followed in the
morning and afternoon by hours of
freedom and recreation, holiday as well
as holy day, and drawing to a conclusion
with an Evensong where lessons and
psalms are chosen for their use and
value to the young, and a sermon
kindling as well as instructive. But the

first responsibility, be it observed, for
the evangelisation of the child does not
rest with the schoolmaster but with
the parents and godparents. Of all in-
fluences the most lasting in life is the
influence of the home, and where that
home is not definitely and distinctly
Christian the baptized child is defrauded
of his rightful spiritual inheritance. Despite the unfortunate fact that our
baptismal service ignores the very existence of the parents, the only rational
justification of infant baptism is the
existence of the Christian home, and
for that, in experience, godparents have
proved for the most part a sorry substi-
tute. Yet so little, apparently, do even
the more educated parents realise their
responsibility that private schoolmasters
inform us of the amazing ignorance of the
children of the wealthier classes when
they join their schools—ignorance not
only of the Catechism but sometimes
even of the Lord's Prayer. Schoolmasters report that it is a rare thing for

a parent to ask any question about the
religion of the school. It is difficult to
conceive of a Christian home without
family prayer, or where father and
mother never speak to their children of
Jesus Christ, and are content to leave
to others the most beautiful and tender
of all parental duties. Without doubt
a Christian home, first and last, is a
home where the Christian life is lived
and its fruits seen in Christian character.
It is the life of the parents which is the
chief educative, and therefore the chief
evangelistic influence upon childhood.
Whatever may be said in defence of our
English reserve in speaking of holy
things, when that reserve prevents
parents from talking freely to their
children about God and Christ, then it
deserves no better name than moral
cowardice and spiritual treachery. Such
parents lose the one influence, did they
but know it, powerful enough to bridge
the gulf which separates their own
generation from their children's. No

parent now has the excuse of ignorance
left him, for the Bishop of Oxford has
provided him with the very thing that
a parent needs to fill in the gaps in his
own religious training, and to put before
him a clear, explicit, and modern statement of the Christian religion.[1] The
evangelisation of the child is best sought
in surrounding that child with a Christian atmosphere in his home, Christian
worship in his church, and a Christian
teaching in his home and in his school,
rather than by the attempt, that has
too often been made by evangelists in
the past, to induce in the child's soul the
anticipation of those great upheavals
and moral storms which in some lives,
but not in all, accompany conversion.
A child's conversion should be the
gradual and calm unfolding of his
spiritual consciousness as Jesus Christ,
his King and Saviour, grows upon his
thought and life. The very idea of
frightening a child into repentance and

[1] Mowbray, *The Religion of the Church.* 1s. net.

confession by the terrors of hell, or by fear in any form, is repellent. The evangelisation of the young must always be a question of religious teaching; a teaching of God as He is in Himself, of the infinite Creator, of God the Spirit, the invisible Presence of holiness and love, of God as seen in Christ with Whose earthly life, so interpreted, the child must be familiar, of duty which will be presented to him not as a dry code of conduct rules, but as the imitation of the living Jesus Christ, of prayer as the free and simple conversation with the unseen Father and Friend, of sacraments as the channels of strength, life, and forgiveness, and as the special treasure of the fellowship of the Church whose existence depends upon them; all centred around the Presence of the divine Lord Jesus. It ought not to be difficult to bring Jesus Christ to the child, for the gospels present the picture of Jesus full of fascination for a child's mind, a picture which only he who

162

keeps childhood in his heart can perfectly retain. Bethlehem, where angels and dumb beasts come to the cradle of the Babe Jesus, belongs to the child-hearted for all time. Which of us has forgotten his early delight in the story of the boy Jesus lost and found in the temple, asking questions while the grave old doctors listen amazed? Was it not delightful as a child to see the love of Jesus for little children, and to hear Him rebuking the too grown-up disciples who thought that the blessing of a baby was waste of time? And how He understood a child's life, its games, its fun, and its naughtiness! He had watched the little Eastern boys and girls playing marriages and funerals, and falling out over their Church play. "We piped and you did not dance, we wailed and you did not beat your breasts." Once when the self-importance of middle-age, the sickness that destroyeth in the noon-day, was creeping upon His disciples, He solemnly warned them that unless

they could regain the child-heart they
could not enter His kingdom. Youth
no less than childhood was sure of His
sympathy. He loved the young ruler
who came with that hunger in his soul
which youth shares with the artist and
the poet, the passion for perfection—
" What lack I yet ? " It was a young
man who interpreted that word of Jesus,
" If thou wouldest be perfect, sell all,"
the little poor man of Assisi. Jesus has
always known how to ask generosity
from youth, in the twentieth century
as in the thirteenth. He has asked it of
ten thousand English lads, and had their
answer though they knew not Who it
was that called them. It ought not
to be difficult to show Jesus Christ
to the young England of our day,
to draw them to His discipleship and
enrol them in His kingdom, for that
kingdom is a kingdom for youth in
its strength. As Jesus dreamed of it,
it was the strong who should take it
by force.

What had I on earth to do
With the slothful, with the mawkish, the un-
    manly?
Being—who?

The disciple who best understood Jesus,
whom Jesus best loved, was the youngest
of them all. Sir schoolmaster, in your
divinity lesson show your young men
Him without whom all education is
vain; show them Jesus, King and
Saviour. Father, as you lead your household worship; Mother, in your Sunday
hour with the children, show them the
true Jesus, the Jesus who never grew
old, the Jesus whose life was one glorious
adventure, the Jesus who still goes
through the world calling for the love
of the young because He loves their
youth. Most of all, show them the
Jesus who is real life, the Jesus who is
still on earth, for the child can understand the Christ of the invisible Presence.
Childhood is full of a rudimentary mysticism. I have seen children at the
Eucharist still and wondering in the

silent minutes which follow the consecration before organ or voice intrude
upon our adoration. Children feel the
atmosphere of the Presence, and their
inarticulate silence is as welcome to
Him as their shrill hosannas. It is by
such experiences that their knowledge
of Him develops, nor will these early
impressions ever be entirely effaced.

XIII

THE WORD IN SEASON

ST. PAUL once charged a youthful bishop to be instant in season and out of season in preaching the word. Succeeding evangelists, possessed of more zeal than discretion, have made much use of this injunction, forgetting that what is good counsel to a spiritual head in his relations to his flock is not necessarily the best guide to an evangelist going to the outside world. Certainly it is no excuse for discourtesy or impertinence, however zealous the zeal which prompts them. Examples leap to the memory of the well-meant follies of a former generation of evangelists. There was the man on the top of an omnibus,

167

or in the railway carriage, who would press the question, " Are you saved ? " or " Have you found peace ? " upon a stranger, and the over-eager tract distributer who would never lose an opportunity of putting a leaflet into the hands of every chance acquaintance. Many a shy man has done violence to his finer feelings in supposed obedience to this apostolic behest, too often with the result that the religion he desired to commend has been brought into derision. Such procedure was very far from St. Paul's intention and utterly contrary to his practice. The apostle of the Gentiles was an astute and tactful citizen of the world. He would seize every opportunity of delivering his message. His own trial in a law-court was for him an opportunity to present the gospel to his judge, but the quick use of an opening is exactly " in season." I cannot find that he ever gave his message where no such opening was afforded him, though his skilful approach,

168

whether to an individual or an audience, gave him the opportunities which he waited for even upon unlikely occasions. Before Felix he begins his defence by congratulating himself upon his judge's long experience of Jewish religion. "I do the more cheerfully answer for myself," and "This I confess unto thee, that after the way which they call heresy, so worship I the God of my fathers," are master touches of judicial appeal before a Roman judge with years of Jewish experience and a Jewish wife. Similarly before King Agrippa, "I count myself happy that I shall answer for myself this day before thee touching all the things whereof I am accused of the Jews : especially because I know thee to be expert in all customs and questions which are among the Jews." But this tactful opening on neither occasion prevented his bold delivery of his message. Felix was moved to offer him a second hearing concerning his faith in Christ, "and as he reasoned of righteousness, temperance, and judgement to come, Felix trembled." In the trial before Agrippa, Paul's defence gave him the direct opening for the most explicit witness to Christ which a law-court had ever listened to. "Almost thou persuadest me to be a Christian," said Agrippa, by no means in irony as Paul's rejoinder shows. Or again, what could have been more winning and arresting than his first words before the university of Athens? "Gentlemen of Athens, I perceive that you are almost over-religious," and the quotation from "one of your own poets." Like Cicero Paul believed in making friends with his audience before he offered them his message. His speech to the crowd on the stairs of the castle at Jerusalem, despite the exciting and perilous moment of its delivery, was a model of the same practised or instinctive skill. The Hebrew tongue secured him an instant hearing, the reference to himself as a pupil of the great and beloved Gamaliel,

" taught according to the manner of the
law of the fathers, and zealous toward
God, as ye all are this day," might perhaps be misunderstood in a lesser man,
as a mere expedient to disarm their
hostility to himself, but what followed
rebuts the slander, and reveals the
evangelist. Never did he tell the story
of his vision in more burning words, nor
bear his witness to his invisible Lord
with grander courage and simplicity.
Only a hero could have spoken the last
sentence of his speech at such a moment
and to such an audience describing how,
while in an ecstasy in the Temple, he
had heard Christ say to him, " Depart,
for I will send thee far hence to the
Gentiles." He could not but anticipate
how they would receive it. " And they
gave him audience unto this word, and
then lifted up their voices, and said,
Away with such a fellow from the earth :
for it is not fit that he should live.
And . . . they cried out and cast off
their clothes, and threw dust into the

air." It is this combination of the courage of a hero with the sensitive tact of a lover which makes the great evangelist. Never in St. Paul did his evangelistic discretion, his courteous consideration for different types of mind, or his careful approach cloak either feebleness, cowardice, or respect of persons. Invariably he spoke out his message, be it appeal, rebuke, or witness, often unsuccessfully, but never without the deliberate effort, begotten of the zeal and love of a great evangelist, to set his message in its most attractive form.

We are not given overmuch, nowadays, to the evangelistic indiscretions of the impertinent question or the tract out of time. Our inclination is more towards moral cowardice and a certain feeble and futile shyness which masquerades as reserve but has its roots in the lack of personal conviction, and our evangelists are more in danger of flattering their audiences than affronting them

172

by intemperate denunciations, but there is still room for improvement in some of our evangelistic methods. What, for example, is to be said for the following incident? By the side of a road leading from a railway station to a huge factory is set a platform. Between the hours of six and seven, many thousands of persons pass hurriedly before it, some hastening to their work anxious to be in time, the rest, after a twelve hours' shift, not less eager to catch their train home to food and rest. Daily, during an evangelistic effort to reach them, speakers are put up to catch the ear of this double stream of hurried or weary folks, whose faces betray their opinion of this preaching out of season. Good-humoured smiles, looks of annoyance or of pity, from most not so much as a glance. The evangelists, it may be said, deserve our respect. They are willing to be fools for the love of Christ. It costs something to mount that platform, and preach to the moving roadway, and

there is some satisfaction to be got out
of trampling on one's pride. But evangelistic efforts are not intended to save
the souls of evangelists. This is to
advertise the failure of the evangelist to
put himself in the place of his would-be
hearers. Ought he not to know that
duty called half his moving stream of
humanity to work and the rest to bed?
The evangelist must begin by placing
himself in the position of those he hopes
to reach. He must learn not only what
are their faults and failings but what
are their thoughts, their attitude to life,
their judgement of other men. Like St.
Paul he must endeavour to think with
their minds. At Woolwich the Cru-
saders were asked a pointed question,
" Have you had a Crusade in the West-
end?" Behind that question it is easy
to see Labour conscious of its new-gotten
power and dignity, keenly resenting the
idea which this class evangelisation
seemed to suggest, that the industrial
classes stand more in need of repentance

than the leisured. No Crusader thought
anything of the kind, but many of our
evangelistic methods betray such relics
of the feudal consciousness. I detect
that consciousness wherever less respect
is shown for the feelings of "the
workers" than would be shown to the
wealthy. To particularise, it is usual
during evangelistic campaigns to ask
leave of the employers to address the
men during the dinner-hour, often while
eating their meal. The men, it is true,
are generally courteous enough to listen,
and some of them to applaud, but if
it is right to ask men of one class to
listen to the gospel during lunch, why
not another? Imagine an evangelist
mounting a chair in the dining-room of
the Athenaeum, " Gentlemen, pray go
on with your meal, but may I ask your
courteous attention for a moment while
I . . ." If it is right to sit down at a
table in the canteen where working girls
are at tea, and politely to engage them
in conversation for their soul's good, why

not the officer on leave drinking tea with
a companion in a West-end tea-shop?
It is true that the working girls display
great tolerance and patience, unless indeed self-conscious laughter gets the
better of them, and opportunities of
helping them may sometimes spring out
of these ill-timed approaches, but differ-
ential treatment of this sort, even if it
occasionally serves an individual need,
rests on a basis of respect of persons
which sooner or later is discovered and
resented. We are bound to respect
personality, and among its inherent
rights must be reckoned its reserves.
An Englishman's soul is his castle whatever be his class. This is not written to
defend the silence of timidity and shyness, still less indifference and unconcern
for the soul of a neighbour. For that
there is but one excuse, the fratricide's
"Am I my brother's keeper?" But I
do desire to suggest a revision of our
evangelistic methods in the light of the
psychology of our own day. Superiority

is the contradiction of the evangelistic spirit and the undoing of the evangelist. St. Paul was the supreme evangelist of the Gentile world because his whole consciousness was coloured by a genuine humility. " Chief of sinners, not worthy to be called an apostle."

We should be wise to refuse all openings which depend upon the permission of masters and employers and not upon the invitation of those we desire to reach, to approach every stranger with equality of respect, to force no closed doors ; and in place of the rough frontal attack upon a soul, which cannot but produce the reaction of self-defence or antipathy, to use the slower methods of human interest in the man as a man. Our divine Lord's approach to the woman of Samaria might well be our guide. He asked a kindly service of her, " Give me to drink," and by that simple request broke through two barriers which separated Him from her : the race hatred of Samaritan and Jew, and

177   N

the exaggerated conventions which among the Jews divided the sexes, and thus He found a way to her sympathy. One by one the flimsy walls of self-defence which she interposed fell. She tries to speak of religious differences, He touches at once the thirst for God which lies beneath all forms of faith and in every heart. It is the woman herself at last who asks His help, and gives Him the opportunity He had sought so patiently, " Go, call thy husband." The soul that we approach must find in us a friend at hand wholly at his service.

Meanwhile night by night the man we want sits in his house. He has few visitors, he is quite willing to welcome the vicar as one, for the parson is still a privileged man though his privileges are passing. He would rather see him there than hear him during the dinner - hour. " If he wanted to see me, he wouldn't call every time when he knows I'm out." We might do worse than revise our clerical time-table and in place of 2.30-5.30 P.M.

read 7 - 9 P.M. "visiting"; and the invitation to return the visit, not at our churches but in our homes, would not always be declined.

XIV

OUT OF THE DEEP

THE Re-evangelisation of England when it comes will come *de profundis*. " This sort cometh not forth but by prayer." We should be guilty of a moral folly, of a futility that would be ludicrous were it not tragic, did we imagine that by naming Committees or by entering upon some scheme of new organisation and external activity, by spectacular advertisement or by well-staged evangelistic efforts, we could secure the return of the millions to the discipleship of Jesus Christ, and the fellowship of His society. On the other hand, it would be only less mistaken to pray and do nothing. Our Lord organised an external embodiment and expression of

His gospel and His grace. It is with us to this day. It is the Catholic Church. But before He chose the Twelve, He continued all night in prayer. Our danger is lest we give more time and place in our thought and concern to external organisation than to the inner spiritual dynamic without which it is impotent. Yet one of my own grounds of faith in the future of the Church of England is in the transformation which is already passing over the action of her Committees. In place of the too often formal and perfunctory Collect, lasting a minute at the most, after which to business, the well-remembered procedure of the past, now any Committee of importance would feel itself at fault, if it made no effort to go apart from the world, and to spend two or three days in silence and communion, as well as in conference, seeking, as those who expect to receive it, the divine light upon their interchange of thought and counsel. Indeed it has already become the custom

for any and every religious meeting to
begin with a space of silence, sufficient
for a recollection of the Divine Presence.
It is a notable gain. Many have been
surprised at the unifying power of such
methods of Committee and Conference,
at the balance and proportion reached
by this corporate thinking, and at its
clear inspiration and guidance. But we
need to travel farther along this road, to
make greater inroads than we have yet
done into old habits, readjusting the
proportion of our time spent in prayer,
silence, and speech. This I do not
doubt that we shall do if our sense of
absolute dependence upon the guiding
of the Holy Spirit continues to increase,
as it has certainly increased within the
last five years. The re-evangelisation
of our land is already beginning to be
recognised as our supreme need ; to be
longed for by many men of all schools
of thought, and indeed of all denominations ; but if it is to be accomplished, the
quickening of the spiritual life of the

182

Church itself is vital beyond all else.
An intensive movement inwards, God-
wards, must precede and accompany
any outward movement of evangelisation. This was one of the unmistakable
lessons of the National Mission. There
are those still who glibly dismiss the
National Mission as a failure, but it has
done more for the Church of England
than its promoters dreamed, though it
has been strangely different from their
expectations. God's ways are com-
monly other than our thoughts. It has
created a new evangelistic consciousness
and conscience in the Church. It has
opened the eyes of the Church to see the
magnitude and urgency of its task; it
has revealed a wealth of evangelistic
resources hitherto unsuspected and un-
used. It did not fill the Churches, but
it has played its part in strengthening
the national purpose in days of crisis
and trial; most of all it has impressed
upon us the necessity of what is inward
and spiritual. It has driven the mind

183

of the Church inwards not only to corporate self-examination, necessary as that was, but to God, to the Christ whose Body she is, whose Presence is her only life. This is a greater gain than any swift and popular success. Christian history is full of warnings of the long-enduring feebleness, and the crop of spiritual disasters which invariably follow a shallow mass conversion of the multitude. It reveals no less certainly that it is only out of the depths of prayer and self-devotion that any evangelistic movement has ever sprung.

In a world of free men, prayer opens a door to the divine entry into the course of human history. In the inscrutable wisdom of God, He neither withdraws nor overrides His gift of human freedom. He forces no entry into the affairs of man. He does not enter from without, like the *deus ex machina* of Greek tragedy, to right a wrong when the things of men are gone too much awry. But prayer, when it achieves reality in

184

free self-surrender to His will, is
God's opportunity. Through the personality of him who surrenders himself
in his prayer to be an instrument of the
divine activity and power, God finds a
way to influence, and mould from within,
the course of man's history. The incarnation of our Divine Redeemer was
no exception to this law of God's working.
That mighty inrush of God into human
life waited upon Mary's prayer and
Mary's self-surrender : " Be it unto me
according to thy will." It was the
immediate and direct answer to the
hidden prayer of Anna and Simeon, and
that circle of seemingly feeble folk who
waited for redemption in Jerusalem.
It would be inconceivable that England's
re-evangelisation should issue from any
other source than these deeps of sacrificial prayer. It is the glory of man that
it is given to him not merely to petition
God for his needs, but himself in his
prayer to become the channel of their
fulfilment. *Fiat voluntas tua* is no feeble

185

sigh of submission, of resignation to the sad but inevitable will of God. It is a trumpet-call which announces the entry of God into the world, and calls to His standard all who will pray that prayer in honesty and truth. To the psychologist prayer is a putting forth of the will of him who prays. He recognises in it one of the real forces that affect life. Will-energy, he instructs us, cannot be lost; somewhere it is sure of its effect upon other minds. He who prays is by his prayer braced, unified, strengthened, and his prayer goes forth from him till it finds some other sympathetic and responsive will which it can reinforce with power. Upon this low level of psychology it is seen that circles of men united in their prayer radiate spiritual energy and fill the land with power, life-giving as the oxygen in the air. But the reality of prayer is infinitely more than this. In the soul of him who prays and in the fellowship of those who unite to pray for some

186

common thing, God Himself is present, putting forth the infinite energy and might of His will through souls surrendered to His purpose to be the instruments of its accomplishment. It is from the infinite deep of God that the power to re-evangelise must spring. So long as our main reliance is upon our own activity we are impotent.

Yet though prayer itself be a gift of God, it is possible to stimulate the desire to pray. The knowledge of need is a well-spring of prayer, and it is within our power to direct the thought of the Church towards its evangelistic task, and to concentrate it upon this primary duty. Concentration is the essential condition of power in prayer. " The very multiplicity," says the Evangelistic Report, " of the demands made upon the Church's thought has distracted her zeal. Enthusiasm divided among too many objects has evaporated. One master motive, seen to embrace all in a single purpose, would make for power."

There is no narrowness of vision here, but rather breadth and proportion. Such a concentration would give, alike to our prayer and our activity, the cutting edge of keen purpose. It would stir to the depths the Church's instinct of prayer, could the evangelistic vision take possession of her consciousness. "In fact," says the Report, "evangelisation includes the whole field of the Church's activity. Kept in the forefront of her thought, it would unify all her operations." It is with the Church as with the individual. The coming of God to the soul in the self-surrender of conversion brings an interior unity. He that has found God, and in God's will the master motive of his life, is no longer a slave to hesitancy and indecision. Here is that which unifies the complexity of life's crowded interests and resolves the discordant clamour of conflicting impulses into the harmony of a settled order and peace. It is so with the Church. War has taught us that

188

it is the great demand that brings the great response. No man can say of the call to re-evangelise England, that it is other than a grand objective.

XV

THE WAY OF MARY

I

IT would seem to be increasingly clear
that it is by individual and personal
influence, an influence which rests upon
the experience of God and the manifestation of His Presence in life, rather
than by mass evangelistic movements,
that our generation is most likely to be
reached. Certainly those movements
which are making converts to-day would
appear to make them by the infection of
personal conviction rather than by public
propaganda.

No more striking evidence was laid
before the Evangelistic Committee than
that of a Nonconformist leader :

" If we could focus all the Christian forces in Great Britain upon getting a saint in every factory in the land and then a saint in every shop and room of every factory, we should see a great turning to God before three years were out." [1]

A new conception of evangelistic work is here suggested to us. We see a vision of the Church, herself rebaptized in spiritual depth and reality, sending out from her altars men and women who would enter all fields of human service and labour, manual toil, skilled industry, commerce, municipal and political life, education, literature, art, music, the drama, with the avowed intention of an absolute obedience to the will of God in whatsoever state of life He calls them to serve Him. It may well be that it is only by heroism and self-sacrifice no whit inferior to the demand of military service, but exhibited in peaceful avocations, that the conditions of our English life will be re-Christianised and England

[1] Evangelistic Report, p. 35.

191

re-evangelised. The letters of Father
Benson of Cowley contain a searching
criticism upon evangelistic methods in
India. He writes :

" I believe that Indian missionaries are
getting generally to feel that bazaar preaching
is of next to no good. Our Lord and His
apostles never carried on a system of what we
now call ' out-door preaching.' Of course in
accordance with the habits of the country their
congregations were often physically out of
doors, but they never preached to haphazard
assemblies. Those to whom our Lord preached
came after Him as I feel assured crowds would
in due time come after a Christian ascetic
known to be settled among them. Reserve
preaches more effectually than parade of any
kind."

The effect of the life of a Christian
devotee would, thought Father Benson,
be more likely to bring the truth home
to the Indian mind " by the repose of a
devout retirement " than the proclama-
tion in the bazaar. " The English must
have some religion," the Hindoo would
say, " for here is one who has been all
these years living here, and he can have

no other purpose than the glory of God."
This was written of India and from the
cloister. England is not India, and we
are bound to allow for the angle of view
from which the good father saw life.
England, though in need of re-evangelisation, is a Christian country, and this
generation has displayed Christian virtues.
Its need is that articulate Christianity
should replace the inarticulate. The
case, therefore, for open-air proclama-
tion of the Gospel in England is clearly
other than in India, and of India Father
Benson hastens to add : " Certainly I
could not recommend mere idle waiting
upon Providence. Prayerful watching
for Providence and careful using of all
opportunities which Providence gives
are sure to be accepted and blessed of
God." But there is here a lesson which
we need to learn if we are to re-evangelise England. It is the summons to
the depths of spiritual reality and prayer.
It is in the power of the Church, if she
will, to foster this interior life, nor is

o

there any greater necessity, for this is
a time in which even outsiders demand
of the Church the signs of spiritual
knowledge, experience, and power for
which the world is in need. Nothing
can be more directly vital to her evangelistic Mission than that the Church
should train her sons and daughters in
the ways of interior devotion. If the
sons of the Church are to be her evangelists out in the world, bold to confess
Christ in daily life, yet doing Him honour
less by what they say of religion than by
a life evidently lived in His Spirit, she
must be ready to train them for their
task, and we shall be wise if we are
willing to learn from every source and
from the many varieties of spiritual
experience by which men have come
into contact with reality.

We need not become imitators, and
we rightly shall exercise a wise discri-
mination as well as an open mind, but
we shall be insular indeed if we imagine
that we can learn nothing from those

194

who are not of our communion. In
Belgium in the years before the war the
institution of retreats for the people
was the means of bringing thousands of
working-men back to Christ and inspiring
them with the evangelistic sense. It
is reported that numbers of these men
coming from retreat had found not only
conversion but the call to be apostles
to their fellows. If in Belgium, why
not in England ? There is nothing de-
nominational or exclusively Roman in
retreats, and if there were, it is the
worth and not the origins of men and
things that matter. The retreat is but
the application of sound psychological
methods to religion, though it was known
to the Church before men had ever
heard of psychology. For a few days
men retire from the distraction of daily
life. They leave for an interval the
whirl of ceaseless occupation, the strain
of toil, and the triviality of amusement,
in order that they may concentrate
their entire thought upon God and upon

195

eternal things. Out of the complexity, distraction, and superficiality of our life in time, they come to the one abiding and supreme reality, to God ; out of the shallows to the deeps, out of the noise of many voices to the silence, out of the strife to that Presence which is rest, out of self to that Will in which is our Peace. And this not in solitude, but in the fellowship of others drawn together by the same desire of God, a fellowship that is assured of a Presence, a fellowship in which as they seek God side by side men help one another in prayer, in sacramental communion, and not least in silence. Concentration, silence, fellowship—these, as we are instructed by the psychologists, are the most powerful of all means to inner harmony and strength. Retreats have been known and used these sixty years by a small section of the clergy ; probably by less than five per cent have they had any regular use ; and by a still smaller section of the laity. The time has come to extend retreats far and wide, to throw them open to all. They must no longer be the privilege of the few, restricted almost to a party. It is time for us to be less careful, it may be, for the Catholic niceties of our own individual preference, and to think only how we may carry to the whole Church and commend to all minds, as well lay-folk as clergy, the essential and the invaluable elements, spiritual and psychological, of the retreat. In retreat hope is reborn into the soul. Thence men return, the priest to his parish, the layman to his daily task, with new and generous resolves and expectations, new courage, new power, new life, for it is the special benefit of retreat that it leads direct to the consciousness of God, and therefore to deeper experience of penitence and renewal.

Something of the blessing of retreat is to be found in the common use of spiritual silence now spreading its healing influence far and wide through the

Anglican communion. It is easy to distinguish two uses in the Fellowship of Silence. The first a silence which waits upon the Spirit, desiring, if it be His will, out of the silence some message communicated through one or other of those present. This in effect is the old Quaker silence. The other, which appears to make a wider appeal to our Anglican temperament, is found to be directly allied to that manner of prayer of which St. Teresa and St. John of the Cross are the great Catholic examples, and of which Father Baker writes in *Holy Wisdom*, the true prayer of silence, the prayer of the will. This silence is sharply distinguished and clearly safeguarded from the false mysticism of quietism by the stress which from the beginning of its use in the Church of England we have been led by God to lay upon the will. This appears in a recent experience of one coming fresh to corporate silence :

" It is just getting deep down into God, becoming aware of God within. It is in no

198

sense passive or negative, rather an intense expectancy, the most wonderful sense of rest and vital refreshment. All barriers seemed to disappear, and I realised something of the one life and the one love permeating all creation."

No student of mysticism could mistake this experience for quietism. It is evident that such a way of prayer leads direct to the deeps, to the quickening of the inner life not only of the individual but of the Church. Such groups of silent prayer spread abroad throughout the Church bring nearer the great day of God's revealing.[1]

II

But of all intensive movements and methods there is none like frequent Communion. The Oxford Movement gave no better gift to the Church than the daily Eucharist, and there is no reason why it should any longer be regarded as characteristic of one school of thought. The strongest evangelical

[1] See Appendix C.

may well be an advocate of daily Communion. He would but be reverting to the first practice of the Church. *And day by day continuing steadfastly with one accord in the Temple, and breaking bread at home, they did take their food with gladness and singleness of heart* (Acts ii. 46).

How close is God to man, how near is Christ in these Pentecostal days! The first disciples knew that they had received His Spirit, and His Spirit was in the most vivid sense His Personal Presence. This is the spiritual atmosphere which surrounds the origins of the Eucharist.

Rightly understood, the daily Eucharist preserves this original element of familiarity and close relation to daily life which distinguished the first use of the Sacrament. It is evident that at the beginning the thinnest line separated the Breaking of the Bread from the common meal. The Lord's table was the table of the household as the bread

200

and wine were the most ordinary food
of the people, and in this they did but
carry on the experience of the days of
the Incarnation. In their intercourse
with their Master they had learnt to
bring together their highest spiritual
experiences and the common things of
daily life; wherever Christ went the
light of the spiritual world radiated
from Him. In the street, by the lake
shore, at the wedding feast, in the
chamber of death, at the dinner-table
they had witnessed supreme manifestations of divine power and mercy, and
the loftiest revelations of God. To the
Jew God was a Being of infinite sublimity yet remote from ordinary life.
He thought of Him as dwelling in the
mount that burned with fire which none
might approach. Unconsciously their
association with Jesus had transformed
their conception of Deity. The transition, therefore, was easy from the familiar
action of their Master, as He blessed their
daily bread, to the Breaking of the Bread

in the Sacrament. Our Lord would
seem of set purpose to have left to His
Church a sacrament which would repro-
duce and extend this principle of His
Incarnation, the highest amid the lowest,
heaven appearing on earth, God in flesh,
divinity in daily life. Stephen Grellet, the
Quaker, was not far from the mentality
of the first Christians when he wrote:

"I doubt very much whether, since the
Lord by His Grace brought me into the faith
of His dear Son, I have ever eaten bread or
drunk wine, even in the ordinary course of life,
without the remembrance of and some devout
feeling regarding the broken body and the
blood-shedding of my dear Lord and Saviour."

It was perhaps impossible that the
Eucharist should retain completely this
familiarity; even before the first age
was over it was celebrated no longer
daily but weekly (Acts xx. 7). The
Corinthian abuses which St. Paul rebukes
indicate early difficulties. The average
Christian man then, as now, could not
live upon the Pentecostal heights. For

the Church as for the individual it is
difficult to maintain the level of our best
moments. The inevitable development
of the Eucharist tended to magnify the
Sacrament by segregating it from common life, and the Lord's table became
sacred and separate. At different times
and in different ways Catholic and Protestant alike have sought to show their
reverence for the Sacrament by rarity
of receiving. But rightly understood
the daily Eucharist is the Church's way
of retaining the Christ-like association
of the highest spiritual act with the life
of every day. It is impossible not to
respect the reverence for the Sacrament
displayed by Presbyterians in their
solemn preparation for its quarterly
reception, but judged by the standard
of the Acts of the Apostles this in-
frequency would seem to have lost sight
of a noble characteristic of the religion
of the Incarnation.

We need not regret Eucharistic development. Life involves growth. The

fondest parent would not desire to retain the child's beauty fixed for ever, at the expense of its progress towards the grander beauty of age, rich in the reflection of human experience and of the glory of God. It is so with the Eucharist. Its development is the necessary consequence of its divine vitality. It may be that the Church has not even yet exhausted the implications of the Sacrament which seems to contain all the wealth of truth, reality, and life that Christ brought to the world. From the beginning the Eucharist was essentially an act of fellowship. Communion and fellowship are one word in the New Testament, but what age since Pentecost so well as our own could lay hold upon the Pauline language, *the cup of blessing which we bless, is it not the fellowship of the Blood of Christ; the bread which we break, is it not the fellowship of the Body of Christ?* (1 Cor. x. 16).[1]

[1] See Dr. Armitage Robinson in Hastings' *Dictionary of the Bible,* article " Communion."

Democracy will one day find its consecration in the Sacrament which affirms that fellowship with man is the condition and vehicle of union with the divine life. A generation which has learnt that only sacrifice can save the world cannot but perceive the truth of a Sacrament which is pure sacrifice, demanding as it does of all who approach the bread of life that they bring body and soul to the altar where the centre of adoration is sacrifice discovered in the being of God. It is small wonder that the men in France find in the Sacrament the satisfaction of their newly awakened spiritual need. They have learnt for themselves that blood shed for freedom is not lost, but avails for the world. The daily Eucharist is the safeguard lest, as the grandeur and completeness of the Sacrament grow larger in our understanding, we lose its familiarity in wonder and awe. It is indeed the power of God, for it is His Presence. It spreads its influence round the world, it penetrates

205

to the unknown land of the spirits departed, yet it is good to hold fast its daily familiarity. Christ brought God near to man, and the Sacrament enshrines that gift. A movement in the direction of daily Communion running through the entire Church would bring men that power to witness to our Lord in their daily occupation which will only follow upon the recognition of the unity of the whole of life.

There remains the depth of pain. We are reminded by the yearly return of Passiontide, and by the spectacle of world-war, that no redemption is accomplished without shedding of blood. In truth England lacks not pain. Though we home-dwellers in this island have not yet " resisted unto blood," though we have had experience neither of hunger nor invasion, yet England, pierced through the soul by the sword of war, mourns stricken at heart for the unfinished lives full of high promise, loved beyond speech, which war has claimed from her. Lost we may not count them. It is our consolation that, in the eternal world which they have entered by the royal gate of sacrifice, they still serve the final victory of light over darkness for which they gave their earthly life, which, as they now behold it, is the healing of their wounds, and in which the stains of earth disappear. Theirs were not the deeps of suffering; that abyss was for the father and the mother at home who find that of a truth they have given all that they possessed, for the young widow as she bends over the cot of her fatherless child, for the girl whom the sword has condemned to perpetual virginity. "If blood be the price of evangel, Lord God we have paid in full." But merely to suffer is neither to redeem nor to be redeemed. Suffering may but harden and embitter life. The evangel must come to the sufferer, the evangel of union through the Cross with Him who alone in history has sufficed by the touch of His pierced hands to give

redemptive power to suffering, and not
only to console the afflicted but to
transmute their sorrow into a well-spring
of health and joy for the world. But
this miracle can only be wrought in the
deeps, in those hidden depths to which,
by our prayer, if we will, under the over-
shadowing of His Holy Ghost, we may
pass. It is from the deep places of our
communion with God, of our secret
self-abandonment to His will, of our
communion with the fellowship of His
sufferings that the power to re-evangelise
England must proceed.

"The ideal which is the ideal of our race,"
says a writer in the *Round Table Review*, "seeks
to embody not only in phraseology and con-
stitutional doctrine, but in the actual conduct
of public affairs so far as the imperfection of
man admits, the spirit and ideal of religion.
Whosoever will be great among you shall be
your minister ; and whosoever of you will be
chiefest shall be servant of all."

Re-evangelisation is the Church's
share in the realisation by our race
of that divine and Christian ideal.

We are sent to a people which has revealed under the drastic stimulus of war an amazing capacity for high service and sacrifice; it is ours to claim those qualities for Christ and for the Kingdom of Heaven. What Church charged with so weighty and glorious a burden would refuse the summons to sanctify herself for their sake? Recently a number of Christian men and women of different religious denominations were drawn together to seek God in silence. An altar lay before them dark in the purple shadow of the Passion. Light fell upon a Crucifix. The stillness of the divine Presence was fallen upon them. The half-hour was well-nigh spent, when suddenly a woman's voice pierced the silence. She seemed to speak with difficulty, with fear, under the evident sense of the constraint of God. This was the burden of the message: "I see vividly before me a picture. It is by a Russian artist; the Way of Martha and the Way of Mary.

To-day the world bleeds from the wounds of war, and the Church is torn by its divisions. Royally has Martha answered to her call, and gone down her road of service ; but the Church, the Churches all of them, have they not been slow to take the way of Mary and to bear the sorrows of the world at the feet of Jesus ? "

Those who heard that voice knew within themselves that God had spoken by His handmaid.

SANCTIFICETUR NOMEN TUUM
ADVENIAT REGNUM TUUM
FIAT VOLUNTAS TUA
SICUT IN COELO ET IN TERRA.

POSTSCRIPT

In their original form these Lent lectures were delivered in Winchester Cathedral and in the Churches of St. Augustine's, Queen's Gate, and St. Mary's, Southampton. The Author offers his acknowledgements to the Editor of the *Church Times* for permission to make use of the reports of them which appeared in his columns as they were delivered in the London pulpit. He has taken full advantage of their present appearance in book form to extend, rewrite, and rearrange them to the best of his power for the convenience of the reader. He was a member of the Archbishop's Third Committee of Inquiry which produced the Report referred to in these pages, and whole-heartedly concurred in its conclusions. But the appearance of the

Report later than had been expected, after instead of before Lent, obliged him to treat of the subject from a more individual and independent point of view than he would otherwise have desired.

Evangelisation is one, whether overseas or at home. The two fields of its activity are mutually interdependent; and if these pages have treated only of the re-evangelisation of England, it is because the writer's own experience has lain exclusively in England and the Empire, and not because he is unconscious of the world-wide range of the Church's task.

APPENDIX A

DR. PUSEY ON FASTING COMMUNION [1]

THAT the danger of over-pressing this rule was realised forty years ago by one of the foremost leaders of the Oxford Movement is evident in the following letter. A more just, balanced, and Catholic statement of the whole question it would be difficult to find.

1879.

I think that the subject of fasting Communion is pressed very unduly upon people's consciences by some, so as to set an ancient custom of the Church against our Lord's command, in some cases.

No one could doubt that early and fasting Communion is the most devotional; the poor feel this. The question arises, when any do not feel themselves sick enough to ask habitually for sick Communion at an early hour, and

[1] *Spiritual Letters of Edward Bouverie Pusey*, edited by J. O. Johnston and W. C. E. Newbolt (Longmans, 1898), p. 273.

yet it is impossible for them to go out without manifest risk of health or life; or (as is often the case in the country) Holy Communion could only be had at a very late hour, with the same risk, though they be well.

I have had letters asking me whether the rule of fasting Communion was so absolute that a person must give up Holy Communion for months together : or from Clergy, whether if they have to celebrate late, they must give up their cure. I have been asked this even by the Chaplain of a Religious House (with which I am not connected). It has been a great practical difficulty. Those who preach or teach the *absolute* duty of fasting Communion, generally preach or teach (as far as they are aware) to those who can communicate early, or where there is early Communion close by. They have no idea of the practical difficulty. It is sewing new cloth on old garments.

Mid-day Communions used to be the rule among us. The early Communions of late years date from the revival of about 1833, except in towns on great Festivals. And it is a difficulty affecting thousands of Clergy throughout the country. I suppose it would, in many cases, be a question between non-fasting Communion and death.

When asked I have been wont to begin at the beginning.

214

(*a*) There is no irreverence in non-fasting Communion, else—

(1) Our Lord would not have instituted it after eating the Passover, for He was Lord of both Covenants, and it was of His own Will that He so connected them.

(2) The Viaticum is everywhere administered after food, but no one would make the last Sacrament an act of irreverence.

(*b*) There is no binding law. I cannot here look over books, but I remember seeing it in the hand of a learned Roman Catholic.

(*c*) It is then a very early and religious custom, originating in such abuses as those at Corinth, yet not without exceptions. Bishop Forbes, who had such varied learning, told me that it had been the custom to allow kings of France and Spain to communicate non-fasting, because it was thought edifying to their subjects to see their kings communicate. The Christmas midnight Mass at some chapel at Rome was or is celebrated (I forget for what reason) an hour before midnight.

(*d*) There is no difference in principle between communicating at the midnight Mass on Christmas night when, *e.g.*, Christmas Day is on a Monday, and on the Sunday full meals have been allowed, and taking food at an early hour on the same day. For the division of the twenty-four hours is of course wholly artificial.

(*e*) In some cases at least there would be a direct conflict between our Lord's command and the observance of the pious custom. Whether the " This do in remembrance of Me " be or be not addressed primarily to the priest, it must include the people. Frequent Communion is the life of the soul : prolonged abstinence would be starvation. The Easter Communion is accounted the very least which would fulfil our Lord's command.

The rigid rule which is laid down by some now, that non-fasting Communion is to be avoided as mortal sin, would in very many cases clash with our Lord's command to communicate.

I wish the young Clergy were less free with the words " mortal sin." It would not, according to their own showing, be mortal sin in their people unless they made it so. For a person cannot fall unknowingly into mortal sin. I suppose they place the mortal sin in contravening the positive law of the Church. I do not believe myself that there is any such positive law of the Church. I wonder whether they themselves think that they commit mortal sin whenever they omit saying the Daily Service. " Mortal sin " is, as you know, what kills the soul at one blow. Do they mean that one who communicates non-fasting kills his soul ? . . .

216

I believe that non-fasting Communion comes under our Blessed Lord's rule, " I will have mercy and not sacrifice," and I feel sure that if He were here He would dispense with the custom Himself in many cases ; as of the weakly. I am certain that He would rather they communicated non-fasting than were starved.

Fasting Communion is, I believe, a pious custom to be aimed at and commended, not one to be enjoined under penalty of mortal sin. This is bewildering to me, and would, I should think, confuse in people's minds the thought of sin altogether.

I need not say that we old Tractarians communicated and communicate fasting, but we cannot lay the burden on the shoulders of the weak or sickly.

APPENDIX B

NOTE ON THE ROMSEY CRUCIFIX BY CANON COOKE-YARBOROUGH

At Romsey Abbey, set in the west wall of the Southern Transept, and close to the door by which for 400 years the Abbesses of Romsey used to enter the church from the cloister, just where the nuns in going about their daily duties would pass and repass continually, stands an ancient crucifix. It is no doubt earlier than the Transept (which was built about 1150), and, judging by the remains of crucifixes at Headbourne Worthy and Breamore, was originally over the west door of the Saxon Church, A.D. 960, which precedes the present Norman building. There is only one other like it in England (at Langford in Berkshire), and it is the most striking example of the *earlier type* of representations of our Lord upon the Cross, which were common from the sixth century onwards, but were displaced by the mediaeval crucifix after the eleventh

218

century. There are three examples of this
earlier type in the British Museum, each in
Byzantine style, and bearing a strong likeness
to the Romsey Crucifix, and in the MSS. of the
Sermons of Ælfric, Archbishop of York (A.D.
990), there is as frontispiece a drawing of a
crucifix almost exactly similar. The difference is strongly marked, and carries us back
to a nobler and grander conception, for the
modern crucifixes present us with the figure of
the Saviour as dead or dying on the Cross.
They appeal to our pity and our gratitude.
" Behold and see," they seem to say, " if there
be any sorrow like unto my sorrow." But the
Romsey Crucifix shows Christ " alive for ever-
more." The head is erect, the eyes open, the
sacred wounds are yet visible, but there are no
nails in hands or feet. Still, there is the Cross
behind to recall the atoning sacrifice, and from
above the Father's hand is outstretched from
the cloud as if to point—" This is My beloved
Son." It is Christ risen and glorified yet
" reigning from the Tree."

The photograph of this crucifix *in situ*,
which forms the frontispiece of this book, is
from a negative taken for the purpose by the
Vicar of Hursley, the Rev. J. R. Husband.

APPENDIX C

SILENCE AND REUNION

SILENT prayer offers a way of spiritual approach to one another, without the sacrifice of principle, to men of divergent views, and may thus have a great contribution to make to the healing of our divisions and therefore to evangelisation. This was suggested in the two books, *The Fellowship of Silence* and *The Fruits of Silence*. Recently news has reached the writer of three interesting experiments in this direction. In Dublin, by the initiative of Professor Trench, silent prayer meetings were held in the Lady Chapel of St. Patrick's Cathedral on Wednesday afternoons during Lent, at which Conservatives and people of *Sinn Fein* sympathies joined together to seek in perfect silence for divine illumination; the majority of these belonged to the Church of Ireland, but by no means all. A letter from a Roman Catholic priest is an illustration of the influence of this venture in the direction of unity of spirit. " You may rest assured that very many Roman Catholics in Ireland send up their fervent prayers . . . for our native land and for the world, and also that there are many who, like myself, long and pray that the day may come, and come soon, when the big mountain that separates us may be entirely removed." [1]

News comes from China of a silent meeting maintained in Peking, which appeals equally to the spiritual needs of Chinese converts and of the Mission workers; while in India there is established a silent meeting, in which daily Christians, Mohammedans, and Hindus join. The story of this remarkable extension is of interest. The staff of a Christian college used to meet daily for silent prayer in their chapel. They received a request from the Christian students for the use of the chapel at this hour, the time of the college interval, to which they at once acceded. Finding that these students used the time for silence, the staff joined them. Recently some of the Hindu and Mohammedan students asked leave to join the silent group, and were not refused. There cannot, indeed, be here the fellowship born of the common claiming of

[1] *Christian Unity in Ireland*, by Dr. Trench (Hodges, Figgis & Co., Dublin, price 2d.).

the promise of the presence of their Master by disciples who meet in Christ's Name, yet short of that bond, the Light that lighteth every man will surely not withhold His shining, nor will the heart of the All-Father be closed to His children bowed in silence before Him.

THE END

Printed by R. & R. CLARK, LIMITED, Edinburgh.

Crown 8vo.   4s. 6d. net.

Tenth Impression.

THE
FELLOWSHIP OF SILENCE

BEING EXPERIENCES IN THE COMMON
USE OF PRAYER WITHOUT WORDS

BY

T. HODGKIN, L. V. HODGKIN, P. DEARMER,
J. C. FITZGERALD, AND C. HEPHER

———————

Crown 8vo.   4s. 6d. net.

Fifth Impression.

THE FRUITS OF SILENCE

BEING FURTHER STUDIES IN THE
COMMON USE OF PRAYER WITHOUT
WORDS, TOGETHER WITH KINDRED
ESSAYS IN WORSHIP

BY

CYRIL HEPHER

MACMILLAN AND CO., Ltd., LONDON.

I

NEW THEOLOGICAL WORKS

THE IDEA OF ATONEMENT IN CHRISTIAN THEOLOGY. The Bampton Lectures for 1915. By HASTINGS RASHDALL, D.Litt. (Oxon.), D.C.L. (Dunelm), LL.D. (St. Andrews); Dean of Carlisle, and Fellow of the British Academy. 8vo.

CHRISTIAN ORIGINS. Articles by various writers. Edited by Dr. F. J. FOAKES JACKSON and Prof. KIRSOPP LAKE. 8vo.

Vol. I. Dissertations on the Acts of the Apostles.

This is the first instalment of an important series of volumes dealing with the early history of the Christian Church.

PREPARING THE WAY: The Influence of Judaism of the Greek Period on the Earliest Development of Christianity. By FRANK STREATFEILD, B.D. Crown 8vo. 5s. net.

BELIEF AND CREED: Being an Examination of portions of "The Faith of a Modern Churchman' dealing with the Apostles' Creed. By FREDERIC HENRY CHASE, D.D., Bishop of Ely. Crown 8vo.

THE FAITH OF THE APOSTLES' CREED: An Essay in Adjustment of Belief and Faith. By J. F. BETHUNE-BAKER, D.D., Lady Margaret Reader in Divinity in the University of Cambridge. Crown 8vo.

RELIGION BEHIND THE FRONT AND AFTER THE WAR. By the Rev. NEVILLE S. TALBOT. Crown 8vo.

THE THREE KINGDOMS: A Young People's Guide to the Christian Faith. By the Rev. F. G. GODDARD, M.A., B.D. With Preface by the LORD BISHOP OF LIVERPOOL. Crown 8vo.

This book has been especially compiled as a handbook for use in the preparation of candidates for Confirmation.

THE RELIGION OF THE BEATITUDES. Based on Addresses delivered at All Hallows, Lombard Street, during Lent 1917. By the Rev. MINOS DEVINE, M.A., author of "Ecclesiastes: or the Confessions of an Adventurous Soul." Crown 8vo. 4s. 6d. net.

INTERCESSION: THE SHARING OF THE CROSS. By CHARLES GARDNER, MURIEL G. E. HARRIS, ELEANOR MCDOUGALL, MICHAEL WOOD, and ANNIE H. SMALL. Crown 8vo.

MACMILLAN AND CO., LTD., LONDON.